90 Devotions on Psalms from

OUR DAILY BREAD®

Songs
of a
Seeking
Heart

DISCOVERY HOUSE
PUBLISHERS®

Discovery House Publishers is affiliated with RBC Ministries,
Grand Rapids, Michigan.

Requests for permission to quote from this book should be directed to:
Permissions Department, Discovery House Publishers,
P.O. Box 3566, Grand Rapids, MI 49501,
or contact us by e-mail at permissionsdept@dhp.org

All Scripture quotations, unless otherwise indicated, are from the
New King James Version®. Copyright © 1982 by Thomas Nelson, Inc.
Used by permission. All rights reserved.

Cover and interior design by Mark Veldheer

Cover and title page photograph © Don White/Superstock

Interior photographs: Page 4 © swisshippo/istock; page 9 © Terry Bidgood;
page 14 © JoopS/istock; page 21 © Terry Bidgood; pages 27–28
© pixelparticle/istock; page 32 © Mark Veldheer; page 39 © RonTech2000/
istock; page 44 © Terry Bidgood; pages 50–51 © Digital Stock; page 57
© visceralimage/istock; page 62 © PahaM/istock; page 69 © Terry Bidgood;
pages 74–75 by Terry Bidgood © RBC Ministries; page 80
© BrianAJackson/istock; page 87 © huePhotography/istock; page 92
© Mark Veldheer; pages 98–99 © ideabug/istock; page 105 © Momo64/
istock; page 110 © HowardOates/istock; pages 116–117 © Mark Veldheer;
page 123 © Digital Stock; page 128 © Mark Veldheer

ISBN: 978-1-57293-827-4

Printed in the United States of America

First printing in 2014

CONTENTS

Foreword by Anne Cetas 5

The Best Teacher 6
Igor and Me 7
What's in a Smile? 8
Early Defense System 10
God, Answer Me 11
Like a (Huge) Diamond in the Sky . . .12
"I Sure Found Out!" 13
God Is Watching 15
Praise for Pressure 16
It Looks Bad .17
Postcard Christianity 18
The Best Question 19
Fair-Weather Warning 20
Sleepless Nights 22
When the Ground Shakes 23
Message from the Skies 24
Forsaken 25
Source of Hope 28
Valley of the Shadow 29
Always with You 30
Regular Checkups 31
Why Worship? 33
No Thanks 34
Our Best Defense 35
Cover-Ups Stink 36
Let's Sing! 37
The Last Jellybean 38
Just You and God 40
The Last Word 41
Joy in the Morning 42
"It Never Touched My Heart" 43
Really Thirsty .45
God's Wheelchair 46
Plenty to Praise 47
Weak Beneath the Surface 48
The Voice of God at Sunset 49
The Wonder of Grace 52
A Fool's Argument 53
Give Him Your Burden 54
When Fear Creeps In 55
Snapping, Snarling Thoughts 56
Filling Up Empty 58
Eat Fast, Pay Less 59
Squirrel Feeder 60
Worship by Prayer 61
Pigs Don't Pray 63

The Other Eighty Percent 64
When Life Seems Unfair 65
Like a Flock 66
Tell the Children 67
Do You Live in a Box? 68
Bull's-Eye 70
Where Are We Going So Fast? 71
Holding On for Life 72
Fresh Fruit 73
Mightier Than All 76
Sustained in the Silence 77
The True Owner 78
Sing Again 79
Just Because He's Good 81
Integrity 101 .82
Five-Minute Rule 83
God's Helpers 84
The Universe Is God's 85
Rescue and Response 86
How to Answer Accusers 88
He Lights the Way 89
I Love You, Daddy 90
In Brief 91
A Bad Day? 93
Follow the Signal 94
From Heart to Heart 95
"I Dare You!" .96
The Forgotten Book 97
The Cheat Test 100
A Fair Trade 101
Beyond the Shadows 102
He Never Sleeps 103
Dying in the Service 104
Keep Laughing 106
We All Need Mercy 107
Rained Out! .108
A Safe Pair of Hands 109
Those Inner Flaws 111
Communion on the Moon 112
Wonderfully Made 113
A Fresh Glimpse of Glory 114
Not Enough Stars 115
Hallelujah! 118
A Lesson in Praise 119

Our Daily Bread Writers 120
Note to the Reader 128

FOREWORD

Y ou might remember the *Where's Waldo?* books from the 1980s. They were popular children's picture books about a little guy named Waldo in a hat, glasses, and red-and-white-striped shirt. He hid in the pages among hundreds of other images that made it nearly impossible to find him. The challenge, which was fun yet frustrating for many children and their parents, was to find him on each page.

We have been created to search for Someone who can't even be seen—God. The apostle Paul said that God made people "so that they should seek the Lord, in the hope that they might grope for Him and find Him" (Acts 17:27). That sounds so challenging that we might wonder if we could ever actually find Him. But the good news is that God is not at all hard to find, for "He is not far from each one of us" (v. 27). He desires to be known and to make himself known to us. We can find Him on every page of His Word. These verses from the Bible tell us that He can be found:

> Seek the LORD while He may be found,
>   call upon Him while He is near (Isaiah 55:6).

> You will seek Me and find Me, when you search for Me with all your heart (Jeremiah 29:13).

> The LORD is good to those who wait for Him,
>   to the soul who seeks Him (Lamentations 3:25).

The *Our Daily Bread* devotional articles and Scripture verses in this book, *Songs of a Seeking Heart*, are meant to help you in your personal search for God as you make your way through the book of Psalms. The articles were chosen to help you find Him. The psalmists who sought Him found that He is gracious, perfect, compassionate, holy, and wise. He is high above us all, yet He wants us to know Him personally because we need Him. Take a few moments in these pages to draw near to God, and He will draw near to you.

Your face, LORD, I will seek.

—Anne Cetas, managing editor, *Our Daily Bread*

The Best Teacher

From the Songbook: Psalm 1

Blessed is the man who walks not in the counsel of the ungodly. — Psalm 1:1

In talking to young people about preparing for the future, I've had several say something like this: "We must get into the world to experience ungodly situations and ungodly people in order to grow stronger."

This kind of thinking has swallowed up many immature Christians and eventually turned them against God. Sure, we're in the world (John 17:15) and we're exposed to non-Christian situations (school, job, neighborhood), but we need to be careful that exposure to those situations does not lead us to embrace ungodly philosophies. All of us would mature faster by following the divine pattern suggested in Psalm 1:1.

First, let's not let our decisions and choices be controlled by the "counsel of the ungodly." Second, we shouldn't put ourselves in a place where those who don't know Jesus can unduly influence our thought processes. Third, let's avoid getting comfortable with those who mock God, His Word, and His role in our life so that their thinking seems right to us.

Trusting the counsel from such sources leads us away from God. Instead, it's best to get our training, our guidance, and our advice from God's holy Word and from people who know it and love it. God and His Word, not experiences, are our best teachers.

—*Dave Branon*

Inside *the* Song

The word *blessed* is sometimes rendered *happy*. We see it translated this way in 1 Kings 10:8 and 2 Chronicles 9:7.

♪ REFRAIN

Delight in God's words, not man's philosophies.

Igor and Me

From the Songbook: Psalm 3

But You, O LORD, are a shield for me, my glory and the One who lifts up my head.
—PSALM 3:3

When I was visiting Siberia to teach some Bible classes, my friend Igor and I stopped at a store. Just outside the door a large, mean-looking dog snarled at us and would not let us inside. After a while the storeowner came out, and to my surprise he shot the dog. So Igor and I went in.

A few minutes later, four angry Russians burst into the building, looking for the man who had killed their dog. One slapped Igor in the face, and another slammed me against a wall. When they saw that neither of us had a rifle, they left. But they returned almost immediately. After more heated conversation, they left again. Only then did I realize that Igor had positioned himself between me and the half-drunken men. They would have had to fight Igor to get to me—and he is one strong man!

What Igor did for me illustrates what God does for His people. King David's foes were aligned against him, led by his son Absalom. Yet David saw God as his shield (Psalm 3:3). This truth reflected David's own relationship to his people. They saw the king as their shield, their protector against the enemy. Now the king saw the Almighty as his protector.

Whoever may rise up against us—man or spiritual foe—will find our God between us and him. We can trust the Lord to shield us from our foes.

—*Dave Egner*

Inside *the* Song

David wrote this psalm while fleeing from his son Absalom. Just when David may have felt abandoned ("There is no help," v. 2), he recognized that the Lord was his shield, glory, and restorer of dignity.

REFRAIN

Feeling down? Look up and let God surprise you with His gracious help.

What's in a Smile?

From the Songbook: Psalm 4

You have put gladness in my heart. —PSALM 4:7

According to an article in the *New York Times*, the act of smiling can promote good feelings. Writer Daniel Goleman cited experiments in which researchers found that saying the word *cheese* caused a person to smile, which in turn created pleasant feelings. On the other hand, saying the word *few* created a different facial expression, which resulted in negative emotions.

Interesting as such a study may be, there's a better way to have peace and gladness. It works from the inside out, not from the outside in.

In Psalm 4, David set forth several courses of action he took when he was feeling deeply distressed. He asked God for relief and mercy (v. 1). He took comfort in knowing that he was favored by God and that the Lord heard him when he called (v. 3). David was quiet before God (v. 4). He did what was right and put his trust in Him (v. 5). He rested in the assurance of God's peace and safety (v. 8). David was confident that he would receive gladness in his heart (v. 7) as a gift from God, not as the result of some forced smile that might bring a temporary good feeling.

Father, help us in our low moments to look up to you. Grant us the peace and gladness that David experienced when he called on you.

—*Mart DeHaan*

Inside *the* Song

The joy of verse 7 is the real deal—and it is directly from God, as contrasted to the temporary gladness of happy circumstances, as the second part of verse 7 addresses.

REFRAIN

If you're looking for joy, look to the Lord and not at your situation.

Early Defense System

From the Songbook: Psalm 4

My voice You shall hear in the morning, O LORD; in the morning I will direct it to You. —PSALM 5:3

Every believer in Christ is involved in spiritual warfare every day. We cannot afford, therefore, to enter the day complacently.

In an article for the *San Francisco Chronicle*, Herb Caen wrote, "Every morning in Africa, a gazelle wakes up. It knows it must run faster than the fastest lion or it will be killed. Every morning a lion wakes up. It knows it must outrun the slowest gazelle or it will starve to death. It doesn't matter whether you're a lion or a gazelle; when the sun comes up, you'd better be running."

British pastor Charles Spurgeon wrote, "If you are not seeking the Lord, the devil is seeking you." We must not wait until we are attacked by Satan to think about the strategy we should use to escape the enemy of our soul. We must seek the Lord early, keenly aware that "the devil walks about like a roaring lion, seeking whom he may devour" (1 Peter 5:8).

In Psalm 5 we read that David expressed his need for God's help. He came to the Lord early in the morning, seeking His guidance and protection (vv. 3, 8, 12).

Let's not move into any new day without being aware of our urgent need for the Lord. Being prepared is the best way to be ready for Satan's attack.

—*Dave Egner*

> ## Inside *the* Song
>
> David's words in this song suggest confidence that God is listening: "My voice You shall hear." This was definitely a prayer of faith.

🎵 REFRAIN

Morning is certainly not the only time to pray, but David's example shows us that it is indeed a good time to talk to God.

God, Answer Me

From the Songbook: Psalm 6

Depart from me, all you workers of iniquity; for the LORD has heard the voice of my weeping. —PSALM 1:2

Theresa left Sue a message that she had some great news. Sue was convinced that her friend had received Jesus as Savior. After all, she had been praying for Theresa's salvation for 30 years. What could be greater news!

A few days later, Theresa revealed her "great news": She had a new boyfriend and was moving in with him. Sue cried out in desperation, "Lord, what makes me think that You would answer me after 30 years of praying?" She proceeded to have a pity party for herself about God's seeming reluctance to answer her.

Some of our hardest struggles are those deep desires that go unmet—when no response comes from heaven for what seems like forever. The psalmist David could relate. He cried, "Have mercy on me, O LORD. . . . My soul also is greatly troubled; but You, O LORD—how long? Return, O LORD, deliver me!" (Psalm 6:2–4). But later in the psalm we read that David knew the Lord had heard him (v. 9).

A month after Theresa's "great news," she called and left another message: "I have wonderful news! I trusted Jesus as my Savior! I don't know why I didn't do it long ago." Now Sue is praying that Theresa will grow in the Lord and seek to please Him with her life.

Keep praying. In His time, God will answer.

—*Anne Cetas*

Inside *the* Song

The psalmist voices a triumphant message. He confidently casts aside "workers of iniquity" because of God's intervention.

🎵 REFRAIN

With God's strength, we can cast aside the negative forces that weigh us down.

Like a (Huge) Diamond in the Sky

From the Songbook: Psalm 8

You have made him a little lower than the angels, and You have crowned him with glory and honor. —PSALM 8:5

Astronomers discovered a star in the sky that has cooled and compressed into a giant diamond. The largest rough gem-quality diamond ever found on Earth is the Cullinan Diamond—at over 3,100 carats. So how many carats are in the cosmic diamond? Ten billion trillion trillion carats!

In our world, diamonds are prized for their rarity, beauty, and durability, and we often hear it said, "Diamonds are forever." But God isn't enamored with diamonds. To Him there is something far more precious.

Thousands of years ago, David marveled at the great value God had set on human beings: "What is man that You are mindful of him, and the son of man that You visit him? For You have made him a little lower than the angels, and You have crowned him with glory and honor" (Psalm 8:4–5).

In fact, God placed such a high value on us that it cost Him dearly to buy our redemption. The purchase price was the precious blood of His Son, Jesus Christ (1 Peter 1:18–19).

If God places such a high value on us, we should also place a high value on the people He has brought into our lives. Bring them before the Lord in prayer. Ask Him to show you how each is more priceless than the most costly jewel in the universe.

—*Dennis Fisher*

Inside *the* Song

Bible scholar Geoffrey W. Grogan says about Psalm 8:5, "Nowhere is human dignity more strongly affirmed than here."

REFRAIN

To be crowned with glory by the King of Glory—marvel at that honor!

"I Sure Found Out!"

From the Songbook: Psalm 9

You have rebuked the nations, you have destroyed the wicked . . . . The LORD also will be a refuge for the oppressed, a refuge in times of trouble. —Psalm 9:5, 9

Bystanders spotted the nine-year-old boy in the swollen river. He was struggling will all his might to stay afloat in the raging torrent. He did not have the strength to swim to shore, though it was only ten yards away. Rescuers jumped in and pulled him to safety. The boy, exhausted and bedraggled, lay panting on the riverbank. After he caught his breath, someone asked, "Did you fall in?" "No," he said. "I just wanted to see how strong the current was. I sure found out!"

Psalm 9 talks about the strength of the all-powerful God, the Creator, Ruler, and Judge of the universe. It describes what happens to those who decide to challenge His strength or exalt themselves above Him. They soon find out how powerful He really is. They lose their thrones. Their kingdoms crumble. Their armies collapse. Yet the Lord endures forever.

The psalmist gives another side to this all-powerful God, however. He portrays Him as the One who protects and cares for those who take refuge in Him. The same God whose power destroys evil preserves what is good. And no one can break through His protection without His permission.

What a comfort it is to know that God's power can thwart the wicked and protect the righteous! I sure can trust a God like that.

—*Dave Egner*

Inside *the* Song

What a contrast this psalm provides! The ungodly risk destruction, but God provides hope and help for the oppressed and needy in times of trouble.

REFRAIN

Who better to anchor your trust in than the One who can provide a safe haven in a storm?

God Is Watching

From the Songbook: Psalm 10

But You have seen, for You observe trouble and grief, to repay it by Your hand.
—Psalm 10:14

As I scanned the newspaper, I noticed that it carried its usual daily share of bad news: Financial woes. Foreign policy concerns. Domestic squabbles. Nothing out of the ordinary.

Then I turned the page and looked into the beautiful face of a smiling teenager. But she will never smile again on earth. An honor student home from college for the weekend, she decided to go jogging with her dog. The dog came home. She never did. Searchers found her body several days later. Murdered.

The story stopped me cold. Not again, I thought. Not another innocent victim. Not another family left to grieve the senseless loss of a precious daughter. Not more dashed hopes and shattered dreams. Why do the young keep dying at the hands of ruthless killers?

> ## Inside *the* Song
>
> How comforting it is to know that God is on the lookout for trouble and, when He finds it, helps us by dealing with it.

I found the answer in Psalm 10. The wicked person does what he does because "God is in none of his thoughts" (v. 4). "In the secret places he murders the innocent" (v. 8), thinking, "God has forgotten" (v. 11). Murder and violence result when people don't think God notices what they do. But God sees, and He will avenge the murder of the innocent (vv. 14–15).

Yes, God is still on the throne. Evil men may think they're getting away with murder, but we can be assured that God's justice will prevail.

—*Dave Branon*

REFRAIN

Because nothing escapes God's view, putting our trust in Him is never blind faith.

Praise for Pressure

From the Songbook: Psalm 11

The LORD tests the righteous, but the wicked and the one who loves violence His soul hates. —PSALM 11:5

A young man was fascinated by a moth and performed a little experiment to see what would happen when it was released from its cocoon without a struggle. Using his pocketknife, he slit the enclosure, allowing the insect to emerge freely. However, it had none of the expected color, it couldn't fly, and it soon died. As he thought about this, he concluded that the pressure exerted on an emerging moth is essential to its proper development—yes, to its very existence! He later learned that through the moth's struggle to free itself, its body fluids are stimulated and the luster is developed on its wings. So too for the Christian, life's pressures can produce positive results.

A dear saint of God, almost a century old, said, "As I look back over my long life, the dealings of God that were bitterest at the time are now sweetest as I remember them and understand His purposes." The songwriter put it like this: "When fierce temptations try my heart, I'll sing, 'Jesus is mine!' And so, though tears at times may start, I'm singing all the time." Most of us must confess we find it difficult to sing in times of sorrow, suffering, and trial. Yet, if we understood that God has a reason for either ordering or allowing every pressure we face, rejoicing would more readily flow from our hearts.

Bitter disappointments, painful suffering, and shattering sorrow, if accepted in faith, can be a means of strengthening our character. What peace is ours when we learn to praise Him for the pressure!

—*Paul Van Gorder*

REFRAIN

Why test God's patience by embracing evil when we know how much He abhors it?

It Looks Bad

From the Songbook: Psalm 12

"For the oppression of the poor, for the sighing of the needy, now I will arise," *says the LORD.* —PSALM 12:5

King David looked out at the world and was troubled. He didn't need the Internet to paint a bleak picture of society or the *New York Times* to remind him of crime and suffering. Even without a cable news show to give him all the bad news, he saw the evil.

He looked around and saw that "the godly man ceases." He noticed that "the faithful disappear." In his world, everyone spoke "idly" to his neighbor "with flattering lips and a double heart" (Psalm 12:1–2).

This description may sound like the theme of a TV show, but it was life circa 1,000 BC. While we may view society's evils as much worse than anything before, David reminds us that evil is not a twenty-first-century innovation.

But David's words also give us hope. Notice his reaction to the bad news he bore. In verse 1, he turned to God and cried, "Help!" Then he implored God with specific needs. The response he got was positive. God promised that because He rules righteously, He would provide protection and safety (vv. 5–7).

When you are discouraged by all the bad news, cry out for God's help. Then bask in the confidence of His assurance. Three thousand years after David, God is still, and always will be, in control.

—*Dave Branon*

Inside *the* Song

God's verbal response in this song is the first such direct answer in the Psalms. It reassures the reader that God cares for those in need and clearly stands ready to assist!

REFRAIN

The more we grow in our relationship with God, the more we will mirror His care for those in need.

Postcard Christianity

From the Songbook: Psalm 13

How long, O LORD? Will you forget me forever? How long will You hide Your face from me? —PSALM 13:1

When my husband and I visited Mount Rainier, one of the highest points in the continental United States, I expected to see some spectacular sights. But for two days the mountain remained shrouded in clouds. So instead of taking pictures, I bought postcards.

Our vacation caused me to question the way I portray my faith to people around me. Do I present a "postcard" view of Christianity? Do I give the false impression that my life is always sunny—that my view of God is always clear?

That's not what David did. In the passion-filled poetry of Psalm 13, he admitted that he couldn't see God and didn't understand what He was doing (v. 1). But by the end of his prayer, he was certain that what he couldn't see was nevertheless there because he had seen it before in God's bountiful care (vv. 5–6).

Christians are like people living at the foot of Mount Rainier. They've seen the mountain before, so they know it exists even when clouds are covering it.

When suffering or confusion obscures our view of God, we can be honest with others about our doubts. But we can also express our confidence that the Lord is still there by recalling times we've witnessed His grandeur and goodness. That's better than postcard Christianity.

—*Julie Ackerman Link*

Inside *the* Song

The psalmist seems to feel like a neglected friend, and it hurts. He longs to see the face of God—to experience a close relationship once again. By the end of Psalm 13, his relationship with God has been reestablished.

REFRAIN

If God were to turn His face from us, would we notice?

The Best Question

From the Songbook: Psalm 15:1

LORD, who may abide in Your tabernacle? Who may dwell in Your holy hill?
—Psalm 15:1

Nobel Prize–winning physicist Martin Perl was asked what he attributed his success to. "My mother," he answered. "Every day when I came home from school, she asked me, 'So, Marty, did you ask any good questions today?'"

David asked the best question of all: "LORD, who may abide in Your tabernacle?" (Psalm 15:1). There are two words ancient Jews had for expressing the question "who?" One is similar to our usage. But David used another word here that asks, "What kind of person dwells close to God?"

The answer came in a series of character traits: "He who walks uprightly, and works righteousness, and speaks the truth in his heart" (v. 2).

It's one thing to know the truth; it's another to obey it. God delights to live on His holy hill with those who are holy—who reflect the reality of the truth they believe. He loves men and women who "ring true."

This psalm, however, is not about any holiness of our own that we think will qualify us to gain entrance to His presence. It is rather about the beauty of holiness that God forms in us as we dwell in fellowship with Him.

The closer we get to God, the more like Him we will become.

—*David McCasland*

Inside *the* Song

This psalm asks: Who can dwell in a close relationship with God? Today, because of Jesus' death and resurrection, all who believe in Him are made holy and can be in a close relationship with Him!

REFRAIN

When we come before the Lord, we need to come carefully, prayerfully, and humbly.

Fair-Weather Warning

From the Songbook: Psalm 16

The lines have fallen to me in pleasant places; yes, I have a good inheritance.
—Psalm 16:6

Adversity can pose real dangers to the Christian. Doubt, discouragement, and depression lurk in the dim shadows of hard times, making us especially vulnerable to temptation and sin. Periods of relative calm, however, can be equally treacherous. Feelings of self-sufficiency can cause us to let down our guard—and that can spell trouble.

Adventurer Harry Pidgeon, who circled the globe in a small sailboat, was asked to relate some of his experiences. He said, "Do you know the most dangerous thing a man sailing alone has to face?" "I suppose storms and rocks," responded the interviewer. "You're wrong," said Pidgeon. "It wasn't storms I was afraid of; but the clear, calm weather when a good breeze was blowing. In a gale when a man goes on deck, he holds fast to something, for he knows he might fall overboard, but in fair weather he's apt to walk around the deck without thinking. Then a little roll of the boat can throw him overboard and he is lost."

> ## Inside *the* Song
>
> Psalm 16:6 holds a certain enthusiasm and exuberance. Why? Because David is celebrating his inheritance—his true riches as an heir of God.

We're not sure of David's circumstances when he wrote Psalm 16, but his heart attitude was centered on the Lord so that no matter what the "weather," he would remain secure. He affirmed his trust in God (v. 1), acknowledged Him as his highest treasure (v. 2), and determined to keep Him uppermost in his thoughts (v. 8).

If you are in a period of life that's free from sickness, financial stress, and other adverse pressures, thank God. But, like David, stay alert! A fair-weather warning is always out when life's waters are calm.

—Dennis DeHaan

REFRAIN

There is no better realization in life than to recall and contemplate your security as a beloved child of the King.

Sleepless Nights

From the Songbook: Psalm 16

I will bless the LORD who has given me counsel; my heart also instructs me in the night seasons. —PSALM 16:7

The psalmist David had his dark, lonely nights when everything seemed out of control. Doubts and fears assailed him, and there was no escape from his problems. He tossed and turned just as we do, but then he turned to his Shepherd (Psalm 23:1) and reminded himself of the Lord's presence. That brought peace to his anxious, troubled soul. David said, "Because He is at my right hand I shall not be moved" (16:8).

We too have occasions of wakefulness when anxious thoughts jostle one another for attention, when we curse the darkness, and when we long for sleep. But we mustn't fret, for darkness can be our friend. God is present in it, visiting us, counseling us, instructing us in the night. Perhaps on our beds, as nowhere else, we may hear God's voice. We can listen to His thoughts and meditate on His Word.

We can talk to the Lord about every concern, casting our care on Him (1 Peter 5:7). We can talk about our failures, our conflicts, our challenges, our anxieties, our frustrations over His lengthy delays—all the things that stress us out and render us sleepless—and listen to what He has to say. That's what can set us apart from ordinary insomniacs. That's the secret of quiet rest.

—*Haddon Robinson*

REFRAIN

Who do you go to in your "night seasons"? Like David, let us go to God.

When the Ground Shakes

From the Songbook: Psalm 18

In my distress I called upon the LORD, and cried out to my God; He heard my voice from His temple. —PSALM 18:6

Several days after a devastating earthquake in the San Francisco area, a young boy was seen rocking and swaying on the school playground. His principal asked him if he was okay, and the boy nodded yes and said, "I am moving like the earth, so if there's another earthquake I won't feel it." He wanted to prepare himself for another shaking of the ground.

Sometimes after a trauma, we brace ourselves for what might be coming next. If we've had a phone call that brought bad news, every time the phone rings we feel panicky and wonder, *What has happened now?*

The "ground was shaking" for the psalmist David after King Saul tried to kill him (1 Samuel 19:10). He ran and hid. He thought death was next and told his friend Jonathan, "There is but a step between me and death" (20:3). He wrote, "The pangs of death surrounded me, and the floods of ungodliness made me afraid" (Psalm 18:4).

David cried to the Lord in his distress (v. 6) and found that He was a stabilizer, One he could trust would always be with him. He said, "The LORD is my rock and my fortress and my deliverer; my God, my strength, in whom I will trust; . . . my stronghold" (v. 2). The Lord will be that for us also when the ground shakes under us.

—*Anne Cetas*

REFRAIN

No matter how dangerous our circumstances might be, our hope and our help are just a heartfelt prayer away.

Message from the Skies

From the Songbook: Psalm 19

The heavens declare the glory of God; and the firmament shows His handiwork.
—PSALM 19:1

The earth's population is now over seven billion. And depending on where we live, finding moments of solitude where we can gaze at the silent night sky is increasingly difficult. Yet, according to the writer of Psalm 19, if we were able to steal away to a spot where the only sound was our heartbeat and the only sight the canopy of the stars, we could hear a message from those heavens.

Inside *the* Song

Bible scholar H. C. Leupold describes the majesty of verse 1 in this way: "It is as if the word *glory* were written in capital letters across the very heavens."

In such a moment, we could hear with the ears of our innermost being the noiseless testimony of God's breathtaking creation.

We could hear from the heavens as they "declare the glory of God" (v. 1). And we could watch in amazement as the sky "shows His handiwork" (v. 1).

We could listen as "day unto day utters speech" that fills our minds with the unmistakable awareness of God's splendid creation (v. 2).

We could marvel through the night as the firmament shows in unmistakable splendor the knowledge of God's handiwork (vv. 1–2).

Our Creator tells us to "be still, and know that I am God" (Psalm 46:10). A great way to do this is to spend time in His creation admiring His handiwork. Then we will certainly know that He is God!

—*Dave Branon*

 REFRAIN

Our universe shouts to us that behind it all is the glorious creative work of our God. Are we listening?

Forsaken

From the Songbook: Psalm 22

The poor shall eat and be satisfied; those who seek Him will praise the LORD.
—PSALM 22:26

Do you know which psalm is quoted most often in the New Testament? You may have guessed the familiar and beloved twenty-third Psalm, but actually it is Psalm 22. This psalm begins with David's poignant, heartbreaking words that were quoted by Jesus on the cross, "My God, My God, why have You forsaken Me?" (Matthew 27:46; Mark 15:34).

Imagine the situation David must have found himself in that caused him to cry out to God in this way. Notice that he felt forsaken and abandoned: "Why are You so far from helping me?" (Psalm 22:1). He also felt ignored: "O My God, I cry in the daytime, but You do not hear" (v. 2).

Ever been there? Have you ever looked up into the heavens and wondered why it seemed that God had abandoned you, or was ignoring you? Welcome to David's world. But for every plaintive cry David expresses, though, there is a characteristic of God mentioned that rescues him from despondency. Through it all, David discovers that God is holy (v. 3), trustworthy (vv. 4–5), a deliverer and rescuer (vv. 8, 20–21), and strong (v. 19).

> ### Inside *the* Song
>
> The language of Psalm 22:26 mirrors that of the feast of the peace offering of Leviticus 7. At that feast, poor friends would be invited to share in the joy.

Do you feel forsaken? Seek the Lord. Rehearse His character. And "let your heart rejoice with everlasting joy" (v. 26 NLT).

—*Dave Branon*

🎵 REFRAIN

We more fully enjoy the gift of God's deliverance from trouble when we share that joy with others.

Source of Hope

From the Songbook: Psalm 23

Is not My word . . . like a hammer that breaks the rock in pieces? —Psalm 71:5

The ancient road from Jerusalem to Jericho is a narrow, treacherous path along a deep gorge in the Judean wilderness. Its name is Wadi Kelt, but it's known as the valley of the shadow, for this is the location that inspired David's Psalm 23. The place itself offers little reason to compose such a hopeful poem. The landscape is bleak, barren, and perilously steep. It's a good place for thieves, but not for anyone else.

When David wrote, "Yea, though I walk through the valley of the shadow of death, I will fear no evil" (v. 4), he was in a place where evil was an ever-present reality. Yet he refused to give in to fear. He wasn't expressing hope that God would abolish evil so that he could pass through safely; he was saying that the presence of God gave him the confidence to pass through difficult places without fear of being deserted by Him. In another psalm, David said that the Lord was his hope (71:5).

Many claim to have hope, but only those whose hope is Christ can claim it with certainty. Hope comes not from strength, intelligence, or favorable circumstances, but from the Lord. As Maker of heaven and earth, He alone has the right to promise hope and the power to keep that promise.

—*Julie Ackerman Link*

Inside *the* Song

Think about these words of author David Roper: "When we come to the end of all valleys, we'll understand that every path has been selected, out of all possible options, for our ultimate good."

REFRAIN

Why muddle along in a seemingly hopeless world when the Author of hope himself has offered to be your Savior?

Valley of the Shadow

From the Songbook: Psalm 23

Though I walk through the valley of the shadow of death, I will fear no evil;
for You are with me. —Psalm 23:4

Darkness upon darkness. Sorrow upon sorrow. Pain upon pain. Anguish upon anguish. That's death.

Death is a fearful visitor, snatching away people who are precious to us and leaving us behind to mourn, grieve, and wonder. It blocks the light that before had shined so freely and easily on our lives.

Whether we're facing the prospect of dying, or dealing with the death of a loved one, death can be devastating. It can sap our energy, change our plans, overwhelm our soul, alter our outlook, test our faith, steal our joy, and challenge our assumptions about life's purposes.

When we walk through the deep valley, we feel swallowed up by the shadow and come face-to-face with fear. The frantic emptiness of our loss threatens the comfort that previously originated from our trust in God, so we grow afraid. Afraid of our future. Afraid to enjoy life again.

Yet in that valley, under that shadow, we can say to the Lord, "I will fear no evil; for You are with me" (Psalm 23:4). His loving arms never let us go. He is always with us.

Slowly at first, but most assuredly, He provides comfort and release from the darkness. He gives light. He leads us out. Eventually, we escape the valley of the shadow.

—*Dave Branon*

Inside *the* Song

At the point of greatest need—in the valley of the shadow of death—the Lord is beside us, comforting and protecting us. He is an escort through life's worst days.

♪ REFRAIN

There is no darkness known to man that cannot be brightened by God's glorious presence.

Always with You

From the Songbook: Psalm 25:4–10

Behold, I am with you and will keep you wherever you go. —GENESIS 28:15

The highway that winds around the southern shore of Lake Michigan can be treacherous in the winter. One weekend as we were driving back to Grand Rapids from Chicago, a buildup of snow and ice slowed traffic, caused numerous accidents, and almost doubled our drive time. We were relieved as we eased off the expressway onto our final road. It was then that my husband said out loud, "Thanks, Lord. I think I can take it from here."

Just as he finished saying the words, our car spun around 180 degrees. As we came to a stop, hearts pounding, we could just imagine God saying: "Are you sure?"

Why do we sometimes try to go it alone in life when at every moment we have access to God? He said: "I am with you and will keep you wherever you go" (Genesis 28:15). And He assures us: "I will never leave you nor forsake you" (Hebrews 13:5).

Scottish mathematician, theologian, and preacher Thomas Chalmers (1780–1847) wrote: "When I walk by the wayside, He is along with me. When I enter into company, amid all my forgetfulness of Him, He never forgets me. . . . Go where I will, He tends me, and watches me, and cares for me."

What a comfort to know that God is always with us—we don't need to go through life alone!

—*Cindy Hess Kasper*

 REFRAIN

You cannot take a better direction in life than to follow the "paths of the Lord."

Regular Checkups

From the Songbook: Psalm 26

Examine me, O LORD, and prove me. —PSALM 26:2

While visiting a neighborhood store, a teenager by the name of Jimmy made a phone call that was overheard by the storeowner.

The conversation went something like this: "Hello. Is this Mr. Brown? I was wondering whether you needed anyone to cut your grass. Oh, you already have someone? Is he doing a good job? He is? Are you sure you don't want to hire someone else? You're positive? All right, then. Thank you. Good-bye."

As the boy hung up, the owner of the store approached the teen and said, "I'm sorry, Jimmy, that you didn't get that job." "Oh, don't worry about that," answered Jimmy. "I already work for Mr. Brown. I was just checking up on myself."

As believers in Christ, we too should check up on ourselves regularly. Because we desire to be approved by our Lord, we should invite Him to examine every area of our lives—our relationship with other Christians, our obedience to the Word of God, and our testimony for Him. If the result of this heart-searching reveals any shortcomings, we should correct them. Doing this on a regular basis will help prevent the consequences of God's disapproval.

Is it time for a checkup?

—*Richard DeHaan*

Inside *the* Song

While Psalm 26 can serve as a checklist of integrity for us, for David, it was a psalm of vindication in which he responds to those who have maligned him.

REFRAIN

Is our integrity obvious to all who know us, especially to God who knows us completely?

Why Worship?

From the Songbook: Psalm 27

Wait on the LORD; be of good courage, and He shall strengthen your heart; wait, I say, on the LORD! —PSALM 27:14

Why bother going to church? Some would tell us that it's better to sleep late on Sunday, eat a leisurely breakfast, and lounge around talking with the family. And then maybe have lunch with friends or enjoy a picnic and games with the children. "Make it a day that's different and even restful," some would say, "but don't waste time by going to church on Sunday!"

Worship? Who needs worship anyway?

We all do! We need worship because we are unique creatures made in the image of God. We are made for God, so we can't fulfill our purpose unless we develop a right relationship with Him. And worship helps us to do that when we focus on the Lord.

As we join with other worshipers in church, our hearts are lifted out of this temporal world into God's eternal world. According to British clergyman William Temple, in worship the *conscience* is quickened by the holiness of God, the *mind* is fed by the truth of God, the *imagination* is purged by the beauty of God, the *heart* is opened to the love of God, and the *will* is devoted to the purpose of God. And thus we are helped onward in our goal of becoming more like God.

Let's decide now that on Sunday we will be in church with a heart prepared to worship.

—*Vernon Grounds*

REFRAIN

We long for God's presence, a reality that is often enhanced by meeting with fellow believers in communal worship.

No Thanks

From the Songbook: Psalm 28

O LORD, my God, I will give thanks to you forever. —PSALM 30:12

While I was teaching at a Christian college, a talented young man pushed his way into my life. He needed one more course to graduate, so he decided that I should give him an independent study in writing. He would be everlastingly grateful if I would just do this—even though it required extra work on my part. The college dean agreed to the idea because of the young man's abilities.

What a headache! He skipped appointments, missed deadlines, and rejected my evaluations of his writing. He turned in the last assignment just hours before graduation.

After all that was done for him, you'd think he would have been grateful. But he didn't express one word of thanks on graduation day or in all the years since.

I don't ever want to be that kind of person. I would rather be like David. When he was in deep trouble, he called out to the Lord for help (Psalm 28:1–2). Afterward, he remembered to give God thanks for delivering him (vv. 6–7). In fact, David's heart of gratitude toward the Lord is evident throughout the book of Psalms.

What about us? Do we have an ungrateful response to the Lord's graciousness? Or are we, like David, unceasingly expressing our thanks to God for His goodness?

—*Dave Egner*

Inside *the* Song

The reason for the psalmist's praise in Psalm 30:12 relates to the beautiful phrase "you have turned for me my mourning into dancing" (v. 11). Deliverance— what a majestic gift from God!

🎵 REFRAIN

Don't let the forever praise of our majestic God wait for heaven— let it begin now.

Our Best Defense

From the Songbook: Psalm 31:1–8

Be my rock of refuge, a fortress of defense to save me. —Psalm 31:2

In late January 1956, during the tense days of the Montgomery Boycott, civil rights leader Dr. Martin Luther King Jr. could not sleep. A threatening phone call had terrified him. So he prayed, "I am here taking a stand for what I believe is right. But Lord, I must confess that I'm weak now, I'm faltering. I'm losing my courage. Now, I am afraid. . . . The people are looking to me for leadership, and if I stand before them without strength and courage, they too will falter. I am at the end of my powers. . . . I can't face it alone."

Dr. King later wrote, "At that moment I experienced the presence of the Divine as I never experienced Him before. It seemed as though I could hear the quiet assurance of an inner voice saying, 'Stand up for righteousness, stand up for truth; and God will be at your side forever.' Almost at once my fears began to go. My uncertainty disappeared. I was ready to face anything."

The rest is history. Dr. King wanted to see people of all colors free of the damage done by racism and prejudice.

If we face opposition when we're trying to do what's right, we too must cry out to the Lord. He alone is our "rock of refuge, a fortress of defense" (Psalm 31:2). He is our reliable source of strength and protection.

—*Dave Egner*

Inside *the* Song

David knew the importance of a "rock of refuge" and a "fortress of defense" as he recalled the times he was pursued by the delusional King Saul. David learned firsthand that his only safety was God.

REFRAIN

When troubles seem to be chasing us, do we seek safety in the world or in the Lord?

Cover-Ups Stink

From the Songbook: Psalm 32:1–5

Blessed is he whose transgression is forgiven, whose sin is covered. —Psalm 32:1

The smell at an overflowing garbage landfill became a growing public concern. So workers installed high-pressured deodorant guns to counteract the smell. The cannons could spray several gallons of fragrance a minute over a distance of up to 50 yards across the mounds of putrefying garbage. However, no matter how many gallons of deodorant are sprayed to mask the odorous rubbish, the fragrance will serve only as a cover-up until the source of the stench is removed.

King David tried a cover-up as well. After his adultery with Bathsheba, he attempted to use silence, deceit, and piety to mask his moral failures (2 Samuel 11–12). In Psalm 32 he talks about experiencing the intense convicting hand of God when he remained silent (vv. 3–4). Unable to withstand the conviction any longer, David uncovered his sin by acknowledging, confessing, and repenting of it (v. 5). He no longer needed to cover it, because God forgave him.

It's futile to try to hide our sin. The stench of our disobedience will seep through whatever we use to try to cover it. Let's acknowledge to God the rubbish in our hearts and experience the fresh cleansing of His grace and forgiveness.

—*Marvin Williams*

Inside *the* Song

How can we not be "blessed," or "happy," as some render this word, when we remember that God not only forgives us through Jesus, but also pushes our sins away—out of our sight—as far as the east is from the west?

REFRAIN

If we hang on to the sin that has been forgiven, we rob ourselves of God's promised blessings.

Let's Sing!

From the Songbook: Psalm 33:1–11

Rejoice in the LORD, O you righteous! For praise from the upright is beautiful. . . .
Sing to Him a new song. —PSALM 33:1–3

Singing has always played a vital role in the worship of God. The psalms were sung in the temple, often in the form of beautiful antiphons; that is, responses between a soloist and the choir, then between the choir and the worshipers. Jesus and His disciples sang a hymn after He had instituted the Lord's Supper (Matthew 26:30). Paul encouraged believers to address one another with "psalms and hymns and spiritual songs" (Ephesians 5:19).

Why should God's people sing? Is it only to prepare worshipers for the sermon? Paul would have frowned upon such an idea because he was convinced that the gospel alone, truthfully proclaimed, is "the power of God unto salvation" (Romans 1:16). We sing because it is an effective way to express our adoration, our supplication, or our testimony. Through song we praise our God and edify one another.

The writer of Psalm 33 called upon the worshiping Israelites to sing praise to God for His powerful word, His unfailing counsels, and His continual concern for His people. Paul and Silas, in prison with their feet in stocks and their backs raw from a brutal flogging, sang because they were filled with the joy of salvation.

> ## Inside *the* Song
>
> If we look back in chapter 32, we read of the psalmist's joy because of the Lord's mercy: "Be glad in the LORD and rejoice, you righteous; and shout for joy, all you upright in heart!" (v. 11). Does our life demonstrate that kind of joy?

If you truly love the Lord, join enthusiastically with others in praising Him through song. When you're all alone and your heart is full, sing! Don't worry about how it sounds. The Lord is pleased with any melody of praise that comes from the heart.

—*Herb Vander Lugt*

♬ REFRAIN

Who better to brighten our dark world than those who display the beauty of God's praise through song?

The Last Jellybean

From the Songbook: Psalm 34:1–10

Oh, taste and see that the LORD is good. . . . Those who seek the LORD shall not lack any good thing. —PSALM 34:8, 10

One afternoon Angela gave her young daughter four jellybeans and let her know that was all the candy she was going to receive.

After practically inhaling the first three candies, Eliana lingered over the final one. She sucked on it, took it out of her mouth, bit into it, sucked on it some more, then gnawed at the outer shell. Knowing that this was her last jellybean, she took a full 45 minutes to ingest the treat completely.

Angela observed her little girl with amusement. It occurred to her that she was watching Eliana learn the value of savoring—enjoying taste and texture and learning to draw out every possible bit of flavor from the pleasurable experience.

When we read, "Oh, taste and see that the Lord is good" (Psalm 34:8), we can be sure that God wants us to "savor" His presence. He allows us to gain intimate and satisfying knowledge of Him. And when we meditate on His Word, we will draw out a deeper understanding of who He is (Ezekiel 3:1–3). As we taste His goodness and love, He will reveal the distinctive flavor of His creativity, sovereignty, holiness, and faithfulness.

Our Father must look on with enjoyment as we learn how to enjoy and savor Him.

—*Cindy Hess Kasper*

Inside *the* Song

The apostle Peter used the imagery of Psalm 34:4 to encourage young Christians to grow in maturity (1 Peter 2:2–3). A growing maturity seems to be at hand for those who taste, trust, and fear the Lord (Psalm 34:8–9).

REFRAIN

Goodness awaits those who dig in and enjoy the presence and the faithfulness of the Lord.

Just You and God

From the Songbook: Psalm 36:5–9

How precious is Your lovingkindness, O God! Therefore the children of men put their trust under the shadow of Your wings. —PSALM 36:7

One spring a pair of blue jays built a nest in the persimmon tree in our backyard. I enjoyed watching the mother bird as she sat patiently on her eggs. In a matter of days, I noticed a new development as I peered from beneath the eaves of the carport. The father would fly in, the mother would perch on the side of that little home, and four little mouths could be seen gaping above the edge of the nest. To get a better look, I would edge closer to the tree. Then I would stand very still and watch the mother. When I got too close, however, she would spread her wings over her little brood. Her head would cautiously protrude as she looked first to one side and then to the other. She was always on guard, protecting her little ones by sheltering them with her wings.

Inside *the* Song

Think about what the word *precious* indicates. When we consider something to be *precious*, it takes on a closeness, an intimacy. God in His lovingkindness is close enough for us to huddle under His protection.

This beautiful picture of protection reminds me of David's words in Psalm 36:7. When he said that we can find safety "under the shadow of [God's] wings," he may have been referring to the words of his ancestor Boaz (Ruth 2:12). Boaz had said to Ruth, "The LORD repay your work, and a full reward be given you by the LORD God of Israel, under whose wings you have come for refuge."

Surely that's a promise we still need. Life is filled with dangers, both physical and spiritual. Yet, we can rest securely because we know that God is aware of them all. We are covered by His omnipotent protection. What better refuge could we have than to live under the shadow of His wings!

—*Paul Van Gorder*

🎵 REFRAIN

No matter the danger or threat, God's wings of protection will never fail to cover us in safety.

The Last Word

From the Songbook: Psalm 38:9–22

But I, like a deaf man, do not hear; and I am like a mute who does not open his mouth. —Psalm 38:13

Walter Heller tells of an experience he had while speaking to the Independent Banker's Association in Denver. In the middle of his talk, a man way in the back suddenly hollered out, "You're stupid!" About five minutes later the man shouted again, "You're stupid!" Heller was irritated. Noticing a slight slur in his voice, he thought, "I'll be ready for him the next time."

Before Heller finished his speech, the man shouted for a third time, "You're stupid!" Heller was quick to reply, "And you're drunk!" The detractor responded, "Yes, but tomorrow I will be sober and you will still be stupid."

Returning insult for insult only makes matters worse. How much better to respond as David did to his enemies! He was sick because he had sinned, and he was vulnerable (Psalm 38:1–5). His loved ones, relatives, and friends had deserted him (v. 11), and his enemies were seeking to harm him (vv. 12, 19–20). Instead of lashing out at them, he turned a deaf ear to what they were saying about him and put his hope in the Lord (vv. 13–15).

Father, help us to be as wise as David. Help us to maintain dignity by trusting you when others take unfair advantage of us. Help us to restrain ourselves and let you have the last word.

—*Mart DeHaan*

Inside *the* Song

There are times when our answer will not effectively silence our enemies. At such times, we can thankfully turn to the Lord and His Word.

REFRAIN

The Lord alone has the answers. What we suggest sometimes gets in the way of truth.

Joy in the Morning

From the Songbook: Psalm 40:1–5

Weeping may endure for a night, but joy comes in the morning. —PSALM 30:5

Angie could not see through the fogged-up windows in her car. Inadvertently, she pulled out in front of a truck. The accident caused such damage to her brain that she could no longer speak or take care of herself.

Over the years, I have been amazed at the resiliency of Angie's parents. Recently I asked them, "How have you managed to get through this experience?" Her father thoughtfully responded, "In all honesty, the only way we have been able to do this is by drawing close to God. He gives us the strength we need to help us through."

Angie's mother agreed and added that around the time of the accident, their grieving was so deep that they wondered if they would ever have joy again. As they both leaned upon God, they experienced countless unexpected provisions for the physical and spiritual care of Angie and their entire family. Although Angie may never regain her ability to speak, she now responds to them with wide smiles, and this gives them joy. Her parents' favorite verse continues to be: "Weeping may endure for a night, but joy comes in the morning" (Psalm 30:5).

Have you experienced extreme sorrow? There is the promise of future joy amid your tears as you lean upon our loving Lord.

—*Dennis Fisher*

Inside *the* Song

As Psalm 40 begins, David is in "a horrible pit," and we can say, "Been there, done that." But he concludes: "You are my help and my deliverer" (v. 17). Weeping weighs us down, but the joy of the Lord lifts our hearts "in the morning" (30:5).

🎵 REFRAIN

As we await the morning joy, our best posture is to sit at our Lord's feet in trust and anticipation.

"It Never Touched My Heart"

From the Songbook: Psalm 41

The LORD will strengthen him on his bed of illness; You will sustain him on his sickbed. —Psalm 41:3

I suppose there are people who have never known affliction. But for most of us, sickness—whether physical, mental, or emotional—crowds into our lives sooner or later. The natural and proper response is to seek relief. The Bible does not guarantee a life free from illness or disability, nor does it assure us that every prayer for recovery will be answered—though many are. But it does promise a spiritual wholeness that is far more desirable than physical health.

This is illustrated by the following story about a handicapped high school student. Although the crutches on which he hobbled kept him from being physically active, he excelled in his studies and was well liked by his peers. They saw the problems he had getting around, and they sometimes felt sorry for him, but for a long time nobody asked him why he had this difficulty. One day, however, his closest friend finally did. "It was polio," answered the student. The friend responded, "With so many difficulties, how do you keep from becoming bitter?" Tapping his chest with his hand, the young man replied with a smile, "Oh, it never touched my heart."

> ## Inside *the* Song
>
> In this psalm, an illness afflicts David—something that relates to his own sin, it seems. Even close friends reject him (v. 9), yet the Lord continues to sustain him.

If you are a Christian who is suffering from a long-term illness that God has not seen fit to remove, don't give in to bitterness, rebellion, self-pity, or guilt. When those emotions well up, as they surely will, be honest with God. He understands. Ask Him to make you a channel for His love and power. As long as you keep your life open to Him, your affliction will never touch your heart.

—*Dennis DeHaan*

REFRAIN

When the cloak of illness darkens our sight, the only unfailing light comes from the Lord of mercies.

Really Thirsty

From the Songbook: Psalm 42

As the deer pants for the water brooks, so pants my soul for You, O God.
—PSALM 42:1

Have you ever been really thirsty?

Years ago, I visited my sister Kathy in Mali, West Africa. During an afternoon of seeing the sights, the temperature had risen far above 100° F. Parched, I told her, "Hey, I need something to drink." When Kathy told me she had forgotten to bring along a supply of filtered water, I began to get a bit desperate. The longer we drove, the more I wondered what it was like to truly die of thirst.

Finally, Kathy said, "I know where we can go," as she drove up to the gate of an embassy. Inside I beheld the most beautiful sight—a water cooler! I grabbed one of the tiny paper cups and filled it again and again. My body had been deprived too long and now required lots of liquid to reverse the effects of dehydration.

The psalmist compared physical thirst with spiritual thirst: "As the deer pants for the water brooks, so pants my soul for You, O God" (Psalm 42:1). His thirst was that of a desperate longing for God—the one and only living God (v. 2).

Do you long for something this world can't provide? This dissatisfaction is a thirst of the soul for God. Run to the One who alone can quench that thirst. "He satisfies the longing soul, and fills the hungry soul with goodness" (Psalm 107:9).

—*Cindy Hess Kasper*

Inside *the* Song

Many things can distance us from God, but the only answer for the great thirst we feel as a result is in searching and finding a place to again "meet with God" and drink in our fellowship with Him.

REFRAIN

Let God feed your soul.

God's Wheelchair

From the Songbook: Psalm 46

God is our refuge and strength, a very present help in trouble. —Psalm 46:1

Jean Driscoll is a remarkable athlete. She has won the Boston Marathon eight times. She has also participated in four Paralympic Games and won five gold medals. Born with spina bifida, Jean competes in a wheelchair.

One of Driscoll's favorite Bible verses is Daniel 7:9, "The Ancient of Days was seated . . . . His throne was a fiery flame, its wheels a burning fire." Seeing a connection between Daniel's vision of God and her own situation, she is able to pass along words of encouragement to others. "Anytime I've had an opportunity to talk with people who use wheelchairs and feel bad about being in a chair, I tell them, 'Not only are you made in the image of God, but your wheelchair is made in the image of His throne!' "

Daniel's vision, of course, doesn't portray God as being impaired in motion. In fact, some see God's "wheelchair" as a symbol of a just God sovereignly moving within human affairs. Other passages speak of God's providence providing help to those who believe (Proverbs 3:25–26; Matthew 20:29–34; Ephesians 1:11).

Jean Driscoll's faith in God has helped her triumph over personal challenges. We too can be confident that the high and holy One is near and ready to help us if only we ask, because that is exactly what we are told in Psalm 46.

—*Dennis Fisher*

Inside *the* Song

God's power is evident in Psalm 46. Here we see that He has power over the elements (vv. 1–30), power over attackers (v. 6), and power over warring nations (vv. 8–9). Indeed, the "God of Jacob is our refuge" (v. 11).

REFRAIN

Don't fear! The God of strength and help is near.

Plenty to Praise

From the Songbook: Psalm 48

Great is the LORD, and greatly to be praised. —PSALM 48:1

God. Have you ever just sat back and marveled at how grand and glorious He is? Today, let's pause to ponder His majesty and greatness.

To help us do that, here are a few descriptions of God that I found while reading Psalms 1–48.

The Lord is a shield (3:3), my source of safety (4:8), my King (5:2), the Judge (7:8), the Most High (7:17), my refuge (9:9), the helper of the fatherless (10:14), the King forever (10:16), righteous (11:7).

God is my strength, rock, fortress, stronghold (18:1–3; 28:1; 31:4), my deliverer (18:2), my support (18:18), my Redeemer (19:14).

He is my shepherd (23:1), the King of glory (24:7), the Lord of hosts (24:10), the God of my salvation (25:5), my light and my salvation (27:1), my strength and shield (27:1; 28:7).

He is the God of glory (29:3), the Lord God of truth (31:5), the living God (42:2), my help in trouble (46:1), the King over all the earth (47:2).

That should be enough to meditate on for one day.

No, that's enough for an eternity! He is "our God forever and ever" (48:14).

Let's start today to worship our God in earnest—the One who gives us so many reasons to praise Him.

—*Dave Branon*

Inside *the* Song

The focus of Psalm 48 is on the greatness of God toward Jerusalem. God has protected His city from its adversaries. We too have reason for praising God, for He is our "God forever" and "will be our guide even to death" (v. 14).

🎵 REFRAIN

The reasons to praise God are as endless as His infinite majesty and greatness.

Weak Beneath the Surface

From the Songbook: Psalm 49:6–15

Surely men of low degree are a vapor, men of high degree are a lie. —Psalm 62:9

In 1835 a man visited a doctor in Florence, Italy. He was filled with anxiety and exhausted from lack of sleep. He couldn't eat, and he avoided his friends. The doctor examined him and found that he was in prime physical condition. Concluding that his patient needed to have a good time, the physician told him about a circus in town and its star performer, a clown named Grimaldi. Night after night he had the people rolling in the aisles. "You must go and see him," the doctor advised. "Grimaldi is the world's funniest clown. He'll make you laugh and cure your sadness." "No," replied the despairing man, "he can't help me. You see, I am Grimaldi!"

Many people are like that clown—weak beneath the surface. The psalmist refers to them as having riches and honor and as giving the appearance of confidence and strength. Yet they lack spiritual understanding and will perish like the animals (Psalm 49:12–14).

We see this even today. People appear to be something they aren't. In front of the cameras, behind the desk, or dressed in their finest clothes, they are pictures of strength. But let's not kid ourselves; we are all made of the same flesh, and apart from the grace and power of God we are helpless and pathetic. Only by yielding to the Holy Spirit can we find the inner resources we need.

Are you displaying His power, or are you wearing a mask that covers weakness beneath the surface?

—*Mart DeHaan*

Inside *the* Song

In verses 13–15, the psalmist contrasts the temporary riches that lead to nothingness with the eternal riches of redemption.

REFRAIN

The things of this world that keep us from God, keep us from true strength and power.

The Voice of God at Sunset

From the Songbook: Psalm 50

The Mighty One, God the LORD, has spoken and called the earth from the rising of the sun to its going down. —PSALM 50:1

Who has not marveled at the beauty of a sunset? We stand motionless, awestruck, hushed by the flaming sky as the sun moves over the western horizon. Seeming to hesitate a moment, the glowing orb suddenly drops out of sight, leaving the sky ablaze with brilliant shades of pink, orange, and red. Somehow the frustrations of the day are put to silence by the majestic, yet soothing voice of God as we view a glorious sunset.

Because the sun's rays are slowed down slightly and bent by the earth's atmosphere, the sun appears to be oval-shaped rather than round. That, along with the dust or smog in the air, explains the dazzling array of colors that give us so much visual pleasure at day's end. And scientists tell us that a sunset can be even more beautiful than most of us have seen. Writing in the *Encyclopedia Science Supplement*, astronomer John B. Irwin said, "When conditions are just right, the last diminishing bit of the yellow-orange sun suddenly changes into a brilliant emerald green. This green flash puts an exciting exclamation point to the end of the day."

> ## Inside *the* Song
>
> As God appears to swoop onto the scene, He is given three designations. He is "the mighty One," He is "God," and He is "the LORD." Contemplate all that this means.

To Christians, every sunset is an exclamation point given to us by God the Creator to end the day. It's as if the Lord were saying, "Set aside your worries. Rest from your labors. Forget about those disappointments. I am still here, taking care of My universe. I am in control. I have not changed. Look up beyond the sun to Me and be at peace."

No wonder the psalmist spoke of the voice of God at sunset!

—*Dave Egner*

REFRAIN

Allow the beauty of every sunset's appearance to be a reminder of God's enduring presence in your life.

The Wonder of Grace

From the Songbook: Psalm 51

The sacrifices of God are a broken spirit, a broken and a contrite heart—these, O God, You will not despise. —Psalm 51:17

When I was a young boy, a few of my friends had fathers who led their families in daily Bible reading and never missed a church service. But I also knew that some of them were proud, tyrants at home, ruthless in their business dealings, and heartless toward people in need. Even as a youngster, I realized that this kind of hypocrisy did not please God.

I was grateful that my father and several other men I knew modeled true faith and humility. They were quick to admit their wrongs and treated others with compassion. They obviously saw themselves as unworthy recipients of God's wonderful grace.

In Psalm 51, David expressed his deep sense of guilt and his desperate need for God's forgiveness and cleansing. As he grieved over his sin, he came to the Lord with the sacrifice of "a broken and a contrite heart" (v. 17). When David thought about God's love, mercy, and grace, he was filled with gratitude and praise.

If we recognize the seriousness of our sin, we too will come to the Lord with the sacrifice of "a broken and a contrite heart." As we consider what Jesus did for us on the cross, taking the full punishment for all our sins, then we will be overwhelmed with the wonder of grace.

—*Herb Vander Lugt*

Inside *the* Song

This penitential psalm of David allows us to listen in as he grieves his own sins and pleads with God for forgiveness. The contrast between David's sin and God's grace is a strong reminder for all of us to keep our accounts clear with Him.

REFRAIN

There is no heart so broken that God's grace cannot heal it.

A Fool's Argument

From the Songbook: Psalm 53

The fool has said in his heart, "There is no God." — PSALM 53:1

Some people spend a great deal of time and effort trying to disprove the existence of God. By doing so, however, they undermine their own arguments. In *Interpreting Basic Theology*, Addison Leitch wrote, "Unless [an atheist] is carrying on his fight against absolute nothingness—and this makes us wonder about his zeal—then he must be [arguing] against something he finds ingrained in himself and in others."

This inherent belief in God doesn't prove He exists, but it strongly hints in that direction. When C. S. Lewis was an atheist, he rejected the idea of a divine Being because of all the injustice in the world. But when he asked himself where he had gotten the idea of justice in the first place, he had a problem. "Man doesn't call a line crooked unless he has some idea of a straight line," wrote Lewis. "What was I comparing this universe with when I called it unjust?" Lewis realized that his case for atheism was too simple. If the idea of justice were merely a product of his own imagination, that would have destroyed his argument, which depended on real injustices. Injustice in the world, in fact, pointed to a God who himself set the standard of justice.

The fool says that there is no God (Psalm 53:1). So be wise instead and make it your primary goal to love the God who is there.

—*Dennis DeHaan*

> ## Inside *the* Song
>
> Psalm 53 closely mirrors Psalm 14. One major difference is in verse 5. Another difference is that God is called Elohim in Psalm 53 and Yahweh in Psalm 14.

REFRAIN

If there were no God, we would have no frame of reference to even consider the need for God.

Give Him Your Burden

From the Songbook: Psalm 55:16–23

Cast your burden on the LORD, and He shall sustain you. —PSALM 55:22

A poor man in Ireland was plodding along toward home, carrying a huge bag of potatoes. A horse and wagon finally drew up alongside him on the road, and the driver invited the man to climb aboard. After getting on the wagon, he sat down but continued to hold the heavy bag.

When the driver suggested that the man set the bag down in the wagon, he replied, "I don't want to trouble you too much, sir. You are giving me a ride already, so I'll just carry the potatoes."

"How foolish of him!" we say. Yet sometimes we do the same thing when we attempt to bear the burdens of our lives in our own strength. No wonder we become weary and overwhelmed with anxiety and fear.

In Psalm 55, David spoke of the anxiety he felt because his enemies were attacking him (vv. 1–15). But then he gave his concerns to the Lord and was filled with renewed hope and confidence (vv. 16–23). That's why he could write, "Cast your burden on the Lord, and He shall sustain you" (v. 22).

When you recall the story of the man and his bag of potatoes, remember the simple lesson it illustrates: Rather than trying to bear your burdens by yourself, set them down in God's hands.

—*Henry Bosch*

Inside *the* Song

Just as Daniel prayed three times a day when he was in exile in Babylon, the writer of Psalm 55 prayed three times a day for God's help (v. 17). We can learn about persistence in prayer through their examples.

 REFRAIN

Our duty and privilege is to transfer our burdens onto God's shoulders. He will sustain us in the midst of trials.

When Fear Creeps In

From the Songbook: Psalm 56

Whenever I am afraid, I will trust in [God]. —Psalm 56:3

When my daughter exclaimed, "Mommy, a bug!" I looked where she was pointing and saw the largest spider I have ever encountered outside of a pet shop. Both the spider and I knew that he would not be allowed to stay in our house. And yet, as I faced him, I found I could not take one step closer to end the standoff. My pulse quickened. I swallowed and gave myself a pep talk. Still, fear kept me frozen in place.

Fear is powerful; it can override logical thinking and produce irrational behavior. Thankfully, Christians don't have to let fear of anything—people, situations, or even spiders—rule our actions. We can declare, "Whenever I am afraid, I will trust in [God]" (Psalm 56:3).

Taking this stand against fear is consistent with the Bible's instruction to "trust in the Lord with all your heart, and lean not on your own understanding" (Proverbs 3:5). Our own understanding may lead us to overestimate the object of our fear and underestimate God's power. When we are afraid, we can depend on God's understanding (Isaiah 40:28) and trust in His love for us that "casts out fear" (1 John 4:18). The next time fear creeps into your life, don't panic. God can be trusted in the darkness.

—*Paul Van Gorder*

Inside *the* Song

In this psalm, David is probably referring to a situation recorded in 1 Samuel 21:12 when he feared for his life at the hands of Achish, king of Gath. He truly was "afraid."

♫ REFRAIN

When fears overwhelm us, we can find refuge in the safety of God's arms.

Snapping, Snarling Thoughts

From the Songbook: Psalm 59

You have been my defense and refuge in the day of my trouble. —PSALM 59:16

Many years ago, my father and I hiked through Big Bend in Texas. It's a national park now, but in those days it was rough country.

One night we were rolling out our sleeping bags when a couple with a dog asked if they could camp nearby. We welcomed their company and turned in for the night. They tethered their dog to a stake beside their tent.

Some hours later my father nudged me awake and turned his flashlight into the darkness. Illuminated by the light, we saw pairs of yellow eyes peering out of the shadows. A pack of snapping and snarling coyotes were closing in on the dog. Although we chased them off and our neighbors put the dog in their tent, we slept fitfully.

I think of that night when I read Psalm 59 and David's twice-repeated imagery: "At evening they return, they growl like a dog" (vv. 6, 14). David was thinking of Saul's army that was closing in on him. I think, however, of the thoughts that return to menace us. They come back at nightfall, snapping and snarling: "You're stupid." "You're a failure." "You're useless." "Who needs you?"

When we have such thoughts, we can revel in God's unconditional, unending love. His steady devotion is our refuge in the dark night of self-doubt and fear (v. 16).

—*David Roper*

Inside *the* Song

This psalm depicts King Saul's dogged pursuit of David. Here Saul's men rise up against David—lying in wait. Like vicious dogs, they come after him. Yet David knows that the Lord is his "defense and refuge in the day of . . . trouble."

REFRAIN

Songs of praise can drown out the howls of our enemies.

Filling Up Empty

From the Songbook: Psalm 62

Do not trust in oppression, nor vainly hope in robbery; if riches increase, do not set your heart on them. — PSALM 62:10

"This house ain't worth robbing," said a thief who seemed to feel he was wasting his time. According to a news report, the burglar broke into a home and held the owner at knifepoint while looking for money. He ransacked the place but turned up only $3 in change, $5 in a wallet, and a few pieces of cheap jewelry.

The thief apparently concluded that the homeowner was worse off than he was, so he gave back to him the $8 he was going to steal. "I think he was disgusted," said the 32-year-old victim. "He couldn't believe that was all the money I had."

We might smile at the bad fortune of this thief. But we can often have a similar kind of experience. It happens whenever we try to take something that God has not given us. Following the path of envy, jealousy, adultery, theft (Psalm 62:10), or just plain stubborn willfulness always results in more trouble than profit.

David, the psalmist, learned this the hard way. When he stole Uriah's wife, he ended up with far more trouble and far less happiness than he had bargained for (2 Samuel 11–12).

Father, help us to believe that it never pays to take what you have not given. Help us not to waste our lives chasing things that leave you out and leave us empty.

—*Mart DeHaan*

Inside *the* Song

Bible scholar Derek Kidner suggests that Psalm 62:10 is referenced by Paul in 1 Timothy 6:17, which says, "Command those who are rich in this present age not to be haughty, nor to trust in uncertain riches but in the living God."

REFRAIN

God's provisions for others are never better than God's provisions for you.

Eat Fast, Pay Less

From the Songbook: Psalm 63:1–8

My soul thirsts for You; my flesh longs for you. —PSALM 63:1

A hotel in Singapore introduced an express buffet—eat all you can in 30 minutes and pay just half the price! After that experience, one diner reported: "I lost my decorum, stuffing my mouth with yet more food. I lost my civility, . . . and I lost my appetite for the rest of the day, so severe was my heartburn."

Sometimes I think in our devotional reading we treat God's Word like an express buffet. We wolf it down as fast as we can and wonder why we haven't learned very much. Like physical food, spiritual food needs chewing! For those of us who have been Christians for a long time, we may have a tendency to speed-read through the passages we've read many times before. But in doing so, we miss what God is meaning to show us. One sure sign of this is when we learn nothing new from that passage.

David's desire was right when he wrote in Psalm 119:15, "I will meditate on Your precepts, and contemplate Your ways." That's the way to treat God's Word—to take time to mull it over.

Let's not come to the Bible as if we were going to an express buffet. Only by meditating on God's Word will we get the most value for our spiritual well-being.

—*C. P. Hía*

Inside *the* Song

In Psalm 63:6, the secret to properly taking in the essence of God and His Word comes into focus: "I meditate on You in the night watches." The word translated *meditate* here has the meaning to not only consider but also to "mutter" or "speak of." It's more than just thinking about God. It's also speaking of Him.

🎵 REFRAIN

Occupy your mind with pursuing God, and watch Him transform your life.

Squirrel Feeder

From the Songbook: Psalm 65

You crown the year with Your goodness, and Your paths drip with abundance.
—Psalm 65:11

Some years ago I placed a squirrel feeder on a fir tree a few yards from our home. It's a simple device—two boards and a nail on which to impale a corncob. Each morning a squirrel comes to enjoy that day's meal. She's a pretty thing—black with a round, gray tummy.

I sit on our back porch in the morning and watch her eat. She plucks each kernel from the cob, holds it in her paws, turns it around and eats the heart out of the kernel. At the end of the day no kernels remain, only a neat little pile of leftovers under the tree.

Despite my care for her, the creature is afraid of me. When I approach, she runs away, taking refuge in her tree and chattering at me when I get too close. She doesn't know that I provide for her.

Some people are like that with God. They run from Him in fear. They don't know that He loves them and richly provides them with everything for their enjoyment (Psalm 65:11).

Henry Scougal, a seventeenth-century Scottish minister, wrote, "Nothing is more powerful to engage our affection than to find that we are [loved by] One who is altogether lovely . . . . How must this astonish and delight us; how must it overcome our [fear] and melt our hearts." God's love is the perfect love that "casts out fear" (1 John 4:18).

—*David Roper*

Inside *the* Song

What a neat picture David gives us of God's goodness dripping abundance upon us—a picture of God's cornucopia of provisions spilling out into our lives—just because He loves us.

REFRAIN

The fear of the Lord is the beginning of wisdom and helps us overcome the fear of everything else.

Worship by Prayer

From the Songbook: Psalm 66

Make a joyful shout to God, all the earth! —Psalm 66:1

When was the last time you and God met together for a worship service? No choir. No piano. No order of service. Just you and God and prayer.

Want an example? Listen to the psalmist: "I cried to [the Lord] with my mouth, and He was extolled with my tongue. If I regard iniquity in my heart, the Lord will not hear. But certainly God has heard me; He has attended to the voice of my prayer. Blessed be God, who has not turned away my prayer, nor His mercy from me!" (Psalm 66:17–20).

Did you notice what was happening in those verses? The psalmist called out to God in praise. He came with a pure heart—cleansed by confession. He was confident that God was listening. God accepted the prayer, and He lavished His love on the person praying. The psalmist's worship included praise, a pure heart, and communicating with God; and then God's affirmation and love were poured out. Yes, true worship took place.

What a pattern! Think of the spiritual advantage you gain and the honor God receives when you practice worship by prayer. Anytime, anyplace, you can worship the Lord, and He will bless you.

Are you ready to worship?

—*Dave Branon*

Inside *the* Song

In verse 5, the psalmist says, "Come and see the works of God" and then recaps Israel's glorious victories from God's hands. This verse applies to our lives as well in so many ways. Come and see!

♪ REFRAIN

You don't have to wait for a church service to stand in praise of our great God.

Pigs Don't Pray

From the Songbook: Psalm 68:4–10

Blessed be the LORD, *who daily loads us with benefits, the God of our salvation!*
—PSALM 68:19

A Christian farmer went to the city on business and stopped at a small restaurant for lunch. When his food was served, he bowed his head and gave God thanks, just as he always did at home. A young fellow at the next table noticed that the farmer was praying. Thinking that he was a little backward and not in touch with "city ways," he asked loudly to embarrass him, "Say, farmer, does everyone do that out in the country where you live?" The earnest Christian turned to him and replied kindly, "No, son, the pigs don't."

The more I observe people, the more I notice that it is the exception rather than the rule to see people bow and give thanks to God in public. We seem to have become a very self-indulgent and ungrateful society.

In Psalm 68, David reviewed the many ways God had cared for His people Israel. After surveying Jehovah's faithfulness, he exclaimed, "Blessed be the Lord, who daily loads us with benefits, the God of our salvation!" From a heart overflowing with love for the Lord, David gave thanks often. Should we not respond in like manner for every blessing God has so freely given? Shouldn't we express to Him our gratitude at all times?

Let's remember to say thanks to God for our daily supply of blessings—even in a crowded restaurant. Let's not be like the pigs.

—*Paul Van Gorder*

Inside *the* Song

Some have translated the phrase "daily loads us with benefits" to mean "daily carries our load." Both are true. God lightens our load of burdens and provides us with all we need— every day!

♪ REFRAIN

If we don't give God our gratitude for what He has given us, what else do we have to offer Him but selfishness?

The Other Eighty Percent

From the Songbook: Psalm 69:29–36

Let heaven and earth praise Him, the seas and everything that moves in them.
—Psalm 69:34

Recently I saw a billboard stating that 80 percent of all life on Earth is found in the seas. That staggering number is difficult to process, largely because most of that life is out of sight.

As I considered this, it reminded me of how much greater God's creation is than we typically appreciate. While we can easily have our breath taken away by a majestic mountain range or a panoramic sunset, we sometimes fail to see His extraordinary work in the details that require more careful study and examination. Not only is much of God's creation hidden by the oceans, but other parts are also too small for our eyes to observe. From the microscopically small to the unsearched reaches of the universe, it is all the work of our Creator. In those magnificent structures—seen and unseen—God's creative glory is revealed (Romans 1:20).

As we grow to understand the wonder of creation, it must always point us to the Creator himself—and call us to worship Him. As the psalmist said, "Let heaven and earth praise Him, the seas and everything that moves in them" (Psalm 69:34). If creation itself gives praise to the Creator, we can and should certainly join the chorus. What a mighty God we serve!

—*Bill Crowder*

Inside *the* Song

Deliverance is in sight for David as he sees ahead to Israel's future. Like him, we can look ahead to see God's ultimate deliverance for us—a rescue that will put us in the ultimate Holy City, New Jerusalem (Revelation 21:2).

REFRAIN

Our inability to see all that God has created should never hinder us from praising Him for all He has given us.

When Life Seems Unfair

From the Songbook: Psalm 73

I was envious of the boastful, when I saw the prosperity of the wicked.
—PSALM 73:3

Have you ever felt that life is unfair? For those of us who are committed to following the will and ways of Jesus, it's easy to get frustrated when people who don't care about Him seem to do well in life. A businessman cheats yet wins a large contract, and the guy who parties all the time is robust and healthy—while you or your loved ones struggle with finances or medical issues. It makes us feel cheated, like maybe we've been good for nothing.

If you've ever felt that way, you're in good company. The writer of Psalm 73 goes through a whole list of how the wicked prosper, and then he says, "Surely I have cleansed my heart in vain" (v. 13). But the tide of his thoughts turns when he recalls his time in God's presence: "Then I understood their end" (v. 17).

When we spend time with God and see things from His point of view, it changes our perspective completely. We may be jealous of nonbelievers now, but we won't be at judgment time. As the saying goes, what difference does it make if you win the battle but lose the war?

Like the psalmist, let's praise God for His presence in this life and His promise of the life to come (vv. 25–28). He is all you need, even when life seems unfair.

—*Joe Stowell*

Inside *the* Song

Isn't the writer expressing what we have all thought at one time or another—that God should, as H. C. Leupold puts it, "reward the godly with tokens of His favor and punish the wicked"? When we get caught up in this kind of faulty thinking, let's do as Asaph did and go "into the sanctuary of God" (v. 17).

🎵 REFRAIN

When we expect nothing more than worldly advantages from God, we are farther from the Lord than we think.

Like a Flock

From the Songbook: Psalm 77:11–20

You led Your people like a flock by the hand of Moses and Aaron. —Psalm 77:20

During a demonstration of sheepherding using a Border Collie, the dog trainer explained that because sheep are highly vulnerable to wild animals, their main defense against predators is to stay together in a tightly knit group. "A sheep alone is a dead sheep," the trainer said. "The dog always keeps the sheep together as it moves them."

The biblical image of God as our shepherd is a powerful reminder of how much we need each other in the community of faith. When writing about the exodus of the Israelites from Egypt, the psalmist said, "[God] made His own people go forth like sheep, and guided them in the wilderness like a flock; and He led them on safely, so that they did not fear" (Psalm 78:52–53).

As part of God's flock, we who have trusted Christ are under His guiding, protecting hand while being surrounded by the shielding presence of others. We are part of a larger body of believers in which there is safety and accountability.

While we don't give up our personal responsibility for thought and action as members of the flock, we are to embrace the concept of "we" rather than "me" in our daily lives. With Christ as our Shepherd and with fellow believers around us, we find safety in the flock.

—*David McCasland*

Inside *the* Song

While God was the true Shepherd who led His people on their wilderness journey, verse 20 reminds us that God used under shepherds along the way—and we can be thankful for their guidance as well.

🎵 REFRAIN

In the church and in the home, it is better to have a flock mentality than to be the lone sheep running a solo mission.

Tell the Children

From the Songbook: Psalm 78:1–8

We will [tell] the generation to come the praises of the LORD. —PSALM 78:4

Imagine an evening in ancient Israel. The day's work is done, the meal is finished, and the family is gathered around a small fire that pushes away the night chill and casts a soft glow on their faces. It's story time.

Father and grandfather take turns relating to the children the "praises of the LORD" (Psalm 78:4). They tell of Abraham's journey. They speak of Isaac. Their voices come alive when they tell about old Jacob. They remember Moses and Joshua and Elijah and the great King David. They recount the history of their own family. And all the time they focus their attention on the mighty works of God on behalf of His people.

That's the way Jewish men fulfilled their responsibility to tell the next generation about the Lord. They had been told by their parents, who had been told by their parents.

Our children need to know about God. They need to learn from us about His love, His faithfulness, and His grace. They need to hear from us about the times He stepped into our lives to protect and provide.

So gather up your sons and daughters and grandchildren. Relate to them how God has worked in your life. Fulfill your responsibility, and tell the children.

—*Dave Egner*

Inside *the* Song

This psalm doesn't present a new concept. Deuteronomy 6:7 is one of several times in the Bible when the Israelites were told to keep telling the story of God to their children—a teaching that definitely transfers to us.

REFRAIN

Sometimes your family's future can be enhanced by talking to them about the past.

Do You Live in a Box?

From the Songbook: Psalm 84

The LORD will give grace and glory; no good thing will He withhold from those who walk uprightly. — PSALM 84:11

Incredible as it sounds, Alexander Whortley lived in a mini-trailer three feet wide, four feet long, and five feet high until he died at the age of eighty. It was made of wood, had a metal roof, and it housed him and all his meager belongings. No matter where he worked, Whortley chose to spend his life in that cramped space, even though larger quarters were always available.

Inside *the* Song

In Psalm 84:11, the psalmist gives a qualifier for God's blessings. Notice the converse of this truth in Jeremiah 5:25 where the prophet warns Judah: "Your sins have withheld good from you."

I can't imagine why anyone would choose to live in a box—certainly not if housing with far more elbow room were available. But are we allowing ourselves to be squeezed into narrow boxes of a different sort? Are we hemmed in by selfishness, an unforgiving spirit, bitterness, or sinful habits? Are we boxed in by unbelief with its coffinlike narrowness of vision, seeing only this little world and this brief lifetime as the hope-suffocating sum of our existence?

God wants us to live in the expansive joy of His strength, realizing the security of His protection and the blessing of His favor (Psalm 84:11). He lovingly urges us to dwell in the spacious mansion of faith and freedom in Jesus Christ. But to do this, we must, in obedience to the Lord, move out of our spiritual boxes and abandon the doubt, the guilt, and the fear that constrict our souls.

—*Vernon Grounds*

 REFRAIN

God deserves, honors, and rewards our obedience. But does He *have* our obedience?

Bull's-Eye

From the Songbook: Psalm 86

Teach me Your way, O LORD; I will walk in Your truth. —Psalm 86:11

If we're not careful, we may become like the man who prided himself on being an expert archer. The secret to his success was that after he shot his arrow at the side of a barn, he painted a bull's-eye around the arrow.

It's easy to live our lives doing what we want and thinking that our ways and instincts are right on target when in reality our "bull's-eye" shots at life are not on target at all. Proverbs 14:12 says, "There is a way that seems right to a man, but its end is the way of death."

Sometimes it may feel right to seek revenge, hoard money, chase pleasure, or yell at people who yell at us. But God's ways are different from ours. He has painted a bull's-eye on forgiving those who have hurt us, on giving generously to those in need, on living to please Him rather than ourselves, and on turning the other cheek. We need to pray, "Teach me Your way, O LORD; I will walk in Your truth" (Psalm 86:11). And then we need to aim to follow His ways in all that we do and say.

But we all need help to aim at the right target. Thankfully, the bull's-eye is already painted in the brushstrokes of God's truth as revealed in His Word. When we aim our lives at God's Word, we'll discover that His ways are right on target—every time!

—*Joe Stowell*

Inside *the* Song

Sanctification is an ongoing process for the believer. Notice that David says in verse 2, "I am holy," meaning a godly person. Yet he still asks God to teach him the way and to help him walk in truth (v. 11). Never stagnant, the God-seeker keeps moving forward in faith.

♪ REFRAIN

Aim high. Aim for God's best. Anything else is off-target.

Where Are We Going So Fast?

From the Songbook: Psalm 90:1–12

We fly away. —PSALM 90:10
My days are swifter than a weaver's shuttle. —JOB 7:6

Scientific measurements indicate that we are moving even when we are standing still. Continental landmasses sit on enormous slabs of rock that slide very slowly at the rate of one to eight inches per year. America is gradually moving westward, away from Europe, at the rate of three inches per year.

If that doesn't blow your hair back, consider this. Our Milky Way galaxy is hurtling through space at 375 miles per second or 1.3 million miles per hour. But that's not all. Within our own galaxy the sun and its solar system are zooming along at 12.4 miles per second (43,000 mph) in the direction of the star Vega in the constellation Lyra.

A man lying on his back in a quiet park on a cloudless day may feel as though all time and movement have stopped under the hot rays of a noonday sun. But the scientist and the godly person know otherwise. Just as we are hurtling through the heavens at unimaginable speeds, so too we are moving from here to eternity. Our days and opportunities to live for the Lord pass so rapidly that we cannot afford to waste time.

Teach us to number our days, Lord. Help us to live without desperation or futility as we travel so quickly from our home to yours.

—*Mart DeHaan*

Inside *the* Song

Spending much time on Psalm 90:10 could be a bit of a downer. The verse reminds us of life's brevity—and the fact that there's a general timetable for us all. But as verse 12 tells us, our short time on this planet has as a goal to "gain a heart of wisdom."

♫ REFRAIN

This life takes on new meaning when we see it as a preview for the eternal life God has planned for us.

Holding On for Life

From the Songbook: Psalm 91

I will say of the LORD, "He is my refuge and my fortress; my God, in Him I will trust." —PSALM 91:2

Try to remember a time when you were in a frightening situation. It could have been a near miss in your automobile, or maybe it was footsteps behind you as you walked down a dangerous street. Perhaps you were threatened by the bully in the neighborhood. Possibly you had to face an angry employer. What about the time you were asked to speak before an audience? In all those situations, did you long to have someone close by to give you support and encouragement?

I remember taking my family to the beach one summer day when the waves were quite big. My daughter Katie wanted to go swimming, but she was afraid of those huge breakers. Only after she realized that they didn't move me, and that she was secure as long as she held onto me tightly, could she enjoy the water and the splashing of those waves. She had someone she could depend on for support.

Psalm 91 describes many frightening situations in which we need the assistance of someone stronger than we are. The psalmist tells us that when troubles assailed him from all angles, he went to One who was as strong and unmovable as a fortress. He clung to God for his very survival, for he had learned that when troubles created waves in his life, he could find security and help in Him.

Are you encountering frightening and unnerving situations? Cling to your refuge and fortress, the almighty God. He's the only one to hold on to—for life.

—*Kurt DeHaan*

Inside *the* Song

We all want safety, and this is exactly what the psalmist offers in Psalm 91:2. Because God is our refuge and our fortress, we have the confidence that no matter what happens, we have a place of safety.

REFRAIN

There is nothing wrong with being afraid, but there is something truly scary about not having anywhere to hide in the midst of trouble.

Fresh Fruit

From the Songbook: Psalm 92

The righteous . . . shall still bear fruit in old age. —PSALM 92:12, 14

I love the old photographs that are often printed on the obituary page of our local newspaper. A grinning young man in a military uniform and words such as: 92 years old, fought for his country in WWII. Or the young woman with sparkling eyes: 89 years young, grew up on a farm in Kansas during the Depression. The unspoken message is: "I wasn't always old, you know."

Too often, those who have had a long life feel sidelined when they reach their later years. Psalm 92, however, reminds us that no matter how old we are, we can have a fresh and fruitful life. Men and women who have been "planted" in the rich soil of God's vineyard will continue to "bear fruit" and be "fresh and flourishing" (v. 14). Jesus promised that "he who abides in Me, and I in him," will continue to bear "much fruit" (John 15:5).

Yes, muscles may ache and joints may hurt, and life may slow down a bit. But inwardly we can be "renewed day by day" (2 Corinthians 4:16).

I recently saw a beautiful white-haired woman wearing a T-shirt that said: "I'm not 80. I'm 18 with 62 years of experience." No matter how old we get, we can still be young at heart—but with the benefit of a well-lived lifetime of knowledge and wisdom.

—*Cindy Hess Kasper*

Inside *the* Song

This passage seems to say that we can be useful no matter our age. Like a tree that still draws life from the soil, an older Christian still abiding in the Lord may have the resources to keep active for Him.

REFRAIN

The key element of growing old is not the old part but the growing part.

Mightier Than All

From the Songbook: Psalm 93

The LORD reigns, He is clothed with majesty; the LORD is clothed, He has girded Himself with strength. —PSALM 93:1

Iguazu Falls on the border of Brazil and Argentina is a spectacular waterfall system of 275 falls along 2.7 km (1.67 miles) of the Iguazu River. Etched on a wall on the Brazilian side of the falls are the words of Psalm 93:4, "Mightier than the thunders of many waters, mightier than the waves of the sea, the Lord on high is mighty!" (RSV). Below it are these words, "God is always greater than all of our troubles."

The writer of Psalm 93, who penned its words during the time that kings reigned, knew that God is the ultimate King over all. "The LORD reigns," he wrote. "Your throne is established from of old; You are from everlasting" (vv. 1–2). No matter how high the floods or waves, the Lord remains greater than them all.

The roar of a waterfall is truly majestic, but it is quite a different matter to be in the water hurtling toward the falls. That may be the situation you are in today. Physical, financial, or relational problems loom ever larger and you feel like you are about to go over the falls. In such situations, the Christian has someone to turn to. He is the Lord, "who is able to do exceedingly abundantly above all that we ask or think" (Ephesians 3:20) for He is greater than all of our troubles.

—C. P. Hía

Inside *the* Song

Interestingly, the psalmist in verse 1 describes God's raiment, not His characteristics. Yet His kingly clothing clearly denotes God's majesty and strength. Perhaps it would have been too much to try to describe God himself.

REFRAIN

Because the One who reigns is perfect and full of glory and strength, His subjects have nothing to fear.

Sustained in the Silence

From the Songbook: Psalm 94:16–23

In the multitude of my anxieties within me, Your comforts delight my soul.
—Psalm 94:19

Hudson Taylor (1832–1905) was the founder of the China Inland Mission and a great servant of God. But after the ferocious Boxer Rebellion of 1900, in which hundreds of his fellow missionaries were killed, Taylor was emotionally devastated and his health began to fail. Nearing the end of life's journey, he wrote, "I am so weak that I cannot work. I cannot read my Bible; I cannot even pray. I can only lie still in God's arms like a child and trust."

Have you been passing through a time when you are tired of body and sick of heart? Do you find it difficult to focus your mind on biblical promises? Has it become hard for you to pray? Don't write yourself off as a spiritual castaway. You are joining a host of God's people who have experienced the dark night of the soul.

When we endure such times, all we can do—indeed, all we need do—is lie still like a child in the arms of our heavenly Father. Words aren't necessary. A comforting father doesn't expect his child to make speeches. Neither does God. He knows we need His soothing care. In times of trouble, His mercy holds us up (Psalm 94:18). We may trust Him to carry us through that dark night of the soul and on into the dawning light.

—*Vernon Grounds*

Inside *the* Song

Some have translated *delights* in Psalm 94:19 to read "soothes." That's a great picture when combined with the psalmist's "anxieties." We need God's soothing, which can turn an anxious situation into a delight.

 REFRAIN

Allowing your anxious soul to be calmed by our merciful God brings true delight.

The True Owner

From the Songbook: Psalm 95:1–7

Let us kneel before the LORD our Maker. For He is our God. — PSALM 95:6–7

Did you hear about the church that didn't have enough room for parking? Fortunately, it was located right next to a store that was closed on Sundays, so a church member asked the store owner if they could overflow into his parking lot. "No problem," he said. "You can use it 51 weeks out of the year. On the 52nd week, though, it will be chained off." The man was grateful, but asked curiously, "What happens that week?" The store owner smiled, "Nothing. I just want you to remember that it's not your parking lot."

It's easy to take for granted all the material and spiritual blessings that God has given us. That's why we need to stop and remember that Scripture says the true owner of all we possess is God: "All that is in heaven and in earth is Yours; Yours is the kingdom, O LORD, and You are exalted as head over all" (1 Chronicles 29:11). Even our bodies do not belong to us: "Do you not know that your body is the temple of the Holy Spirit . . . and you are not your own? For you were bought at a price" (1 Corinthians 6:19–20).

As 1 Timothy 6:17 reminds us: "God . . . gives us richly all things to enjoy." We are so abundantly blessed with good things! Let's never take our Father for granted, but use wisely and gratefully all that He has given us.

— *Cindy Hess Kasper*

Inside *the* Song

In Psalm 95:6, the writer makes three references to a position of humility before God: "bow down," "kneel," and "worship." Clearly, we must come before God with this attitude.

REFRAIN

If our attitude is one of gratitude, our worship will demonstrate God's "worth-ship."

Sing Again

From the Songbook: Psalm 96

Oh, sing to the LORD a new song! Sing to the LORD, all the earth. Sing to the LORD, bless His name. —PSALM 96:1–2

As part of a campaign called "Get America Singing . . . Again," a group of music educators published a list of 42 songs that it feels Americans must continue singing to preserve an important part of the national culture. The list begins alphabetically with "Amazing Grace" and ends with "Zip-A-Dee-Doo-Dah." The group's president said, "We have a whole generation that has grown up without singing songs like these—songs that are . . . part of who we are."

Not only in the United States, but also in every country and culture, music is an important part of who people are.

As Christians, we have a wonderful heritage of music. I enjoy using a hymnbook along with the Bible during my time of daily reading and prayer. Sometimes words written many years ago bring a fresh message of hope. I may encounter a familiar song that sparks a memory of God's faithfulness or rekindles a flame of devotion. More than a memory of the past, it becomes a vehicle to praise God today.

Psalm 96:2 encourages us to "sing to the Lord, bless His name; proclaim the good news of His salvation from day to day." Why not open that long-neglected hymnbook today, rediscover some marvelous messages of faith, and sing . . . again!

—*David McCasland*

Inside *the* Song

When you have a favorite song, doesn't each time seem like you are singing it in a fresh and new way? That's the idea of Psalm 96:1. It's really not a new idea—it's a new recounting of the one great story!

♪ REFRAIN

Whether it's the original "Amazing Grace" or the newer "Amazing Grace, My Chains Are Gone," it's the grace that's amazing—not the arrangement.

Just Because He's Good

From the Songbook: Psalm 100

The LORD is good; His mercy is everlasting, and His truth endures to all generations. —PSALM 100:5

Joel and Lauren decided to move from Washington State back home to Michigan. Wanting to make one last special memory, they bought coffee from their favorite cafe and then stopped at their favorite bookstore. There they picked up two bumper stickers with a favorite motto of the town they were saying good-bye to: "It's an Edmonds kind of day."

After two weeks and a 3,000-mile drive, they entered Michigan. Hungry and wanting to celebrate their arrival, they stopped and asked about where to find a restaurant. Although they had to backtrack a few miles, they found a quaint little cafe. Emma, their waitress, excited to learn they were from her home state of Washington, asked, "What city?" "Edmonds," they replied. "That's where I'm from!" she said. Wanting to share the joy, Joel got their extra bumper sticker from the car and handed it to her. Amazingly, the sticker was from her mother's store! It had gone from her mom's hands to theirs, across 3,000 miles, to her hands.

Mere coincidence? Or were these experiences good gifts orchestrated by a good God who loves to encourage His children? Proverbs tells us, "A man's steps are directed by the LORD" (20:24 NIV). In response, let's "bless His name. For the LORD is good" (Psalm 100:4–5).

—*Anne Cetas*

Inside *the* Song

There's an important theology lesson in Psalm 100:5: God is good, God is eternally merciful, and God's truth endures forever. That's quite a lesson!

REFRAIN

Looking for guidance? Look to the One who sees all and knows all—and made it all.

Integrity 101

From the Songbook: Psalm 101

What may be known of God is manifest in them, for God has shown it to them.
—PSALM 101:2

Officials in Philadelphia were astonished to receive a letter and payment from a motorist who had been given a speeding ticket in 1954. John Gedge, an English tourist, had been visiting the City of Brotherly Love when he was cited for speeding. The penalty was $15, but Gedge forgot about the ticket for almost 52 years until he discovered it in an old coat. "I thought, I've got to pay it," said Gedge, 84, who lived in a nursing home in East Sussex when he decided to pay up. "Englishmen pay their debts. My conscience is clear."

This story reminded me of the psalmist David's commitment to integrity. Although he made some terrible choices in his life, Psalm 101 declares his resolve to live blamelessly. His integrity would begin in the privacy of his own house (v. 2) and extend to his choice of colleagues and friends (vv. 6–7). In sharp contrast to the corrupt lives of most kings of the ancient Near East, David's integrity led him to respect the life of his sworn enemy, King Saul (1 Samuel 24:4–6; 26:8–9).

As followers of Jesus, we are called to walk in integrity and to maintain a clear conscience. When we honor our commitments to God and to others, we will walk in fellowship with God. Our integrity will guide us (Proverbs 11:3) and help us walk securely (10:9).

—*Marvin Williams*

Inside *the* Song

As David writes—and as he found out to his own undoing—it is at home where the heart should shine the brightest in its straightforwardness. It's hard to miss the irony of David's words in verse 2.

REFRAIN

The path of integrity takes us past the pitfalls of distrust and a damaged reputation.

Five-Minute Rule

From the Songbook: Psalm 102

He shall regard the prayer of the destitute, and shall not despise their prayer.
—Psalm 102:17

I read about a five-minute rule that a mother had for her children. They had to be ready for school and gather together five minutes before it was time to leave each day.

They would gather around Mom, and she would pray for each one by name, asking for the Lord's blessing on their day. Then she'd give them a kiss and off they'd run. Even neighborhood kids would be included in the prayer circle if they happened to stop by. One of the children said many years later that she learned from this experience how crucial prayer is to her day.

The writer of Psalm 102 knew the importance of prayer. This psalm is labeled, "A prayer of the afflicted, when he is overwhelmed and pours out his complaint before the Lord." He cried out, "Hear my prayer, O Lord . . . ; in the day that I call, answer me speedily" (vv. 1–2). God looks down "from the height of His sanctuary; from heaven [He views] the earth" (v. 19).

God cares for you and wants to hear from you. Whether you follow the five-minute rule asking for blessings on the day or need to spend more time crying out to Him in deep distress, talk to the Lord each day. Your example may have a big impact on your family or someone close to you.

—*Anne Cetas*

Inside *the* Song

The psalmist, while decrying the state of things in Zion, knows that God can restore. He can even restore the "destitute" (v. 17). Ever been there? If so, this verse is for you.

REFRAIN

It's a compassionate God—a God of all comfort—who listens to your prayer of despair and responds with love.

God's Helpers

From the Songbook: Psalm 103:19–22

Bless the LORD, you His angels. —Psalm 103:20

I was having a conversation with some children about God and superheroes when Tobias asked a question. An imaginative, curious five-year-old, he asked anyone listening: "Does God have a sidekick like Hercules does?" His wiser, older brother, age seven, quickly responded: "Yes, He has thousands of them—they're His angels."

Angels are a popular topic of discussion, and people believe a number of myths about them. For instance, some people pray to angels, thinking they are on the same level as God himself. And some believe that people become angels when they die. But here's what the Bible, our authority, teaches:

- God created angels (Colossians 1:15–17).
- Angels worship God (Nehemiah 9:6) and are known by these terms: archangels (Jude 1:9), cherubim (2 Kings 19:15), and seraphim (Isaiah 6:1–3).
- They minister to God's people (Hebrews 1:13–14) by guarding and protecting them (Psalm 91:9–12).
- They are given special assignments by God (Matthew 1:20; Luke 1:26).
- God's angels rejoice when we repent of sin and turn to Christ for salvation (Luke 15:7, 10).

Only God deserves our worship. So let's join the angels in singing His praises!

—*Anne Cetas*

Inside *the* Song

Here's different admonition to praise God. If God's heavenly hosts— His angels—are called to bless God, then shouldn't we do the same?

REFRAIN

We do the work of the angels when we sing the praises of the One who made them—and us.

The Universe Is God's

From the Songbook: Psalm 104:31–35

He touches the hills, and they smoke. —Psalm 104:32

Rising 6.3 miles from its base on the ocean floor and stretching 75 miles across, Hawaii's Mauna Loa is the largest volcano on Earth. But on the surface of the planet Mars stands Olympus Mons, the largest volcano yet discovered in our solar system. The altitude of Olympus Mons is three times higher than Mt. Everest and a hundred times more massive than Mauna Loa. It's large enough to contain the entire chain of the Hawaiian Islands!

Long ago, David looked up at the night skies and stood in awe at the wonder of his Creator's universe. He wrote, "The heavens declare the glory of God; and the firmament shows His handiwork" (Psalm 19:1).

But the stars and the sky were not all that stirred the wonder of ancient writers. Earthquakes and volcanoes also inspired awe for the Creator. Psalm 104 says, "[God] looks on the earth, and it trembles; He touches the hills, and they smoke" (v. 32).

As space probes explore more of our solar system, they will continue to discover unknown wonders. But whatever they find is the work of the same Creator (Genesis 1:1).

The wonders of the universe should move us to praise God, just as they moved a shepherd boy long ago as he gazed up at the heavens (Psalm 8:3–5).

—M. R. DeHaan

Inside *the* Song

While we normally associate such phenomena as volcanoes with the natural reaction of the elements inside the mountain, Psalm 104:32 seems to indicate that God's hand is a part of these events as well.

REFRAIN

It doesn't take a rejection of science to recognize God's role in this majestic world He created, organized, and superintends.

Rescue and Response

From the Songbook: Psalm 107:1–9

Let the redeemed of the LORD say so, whom He has redeemed from the hand of the enemy. —PSALM 107:2

The sign outside Dave James's shop in Seattle, Washington, says more about getting your life repaired than it does about fixing your vacuum cleaner, but Dave is in business to do both. The top line of the sign is always the same: Free Bibles Inside. The second line changes and features thoughts such as: Surrender Your Heart for a Brand-New Start.

Over the past decade, Mr. James has repaired thousands of vacuum cleaners and given away thousands of Bibles to his customers. It's his way of saying thanks to the Lord for saving him from destruction.

As a successful businessman, Dave James had slipped into a life of drug addiction. "If God hadn't taken cocaine away from me," he says, "I'd be dead." The Lord helped him get clean and find a new beginning.

Every testimony for Christ begins with a rescue followed by a thankful response: "Oh, give thanks to the LORD, for He is good! For His mercy endures forever" (Psalm 107:1).

Whether our experience of salvation sounds dramatic or not, the reality remains: "He has delivered us from the power of darkness and conveyed us into the kingdom of the Son of His love" (Colossians 1:13). Because we have been redeemed, we should want to tell others.

—*David McCasland*

Inside *the* Song

In Psalm 107:2 we read the word *redeemed* one way; the folks to whom it was originally written saw something else. They were redeemed out of Egypt and given a Promised Land east of the Jordan. We've been redeemed from sin and given a Promised Land in heaven. And we need to "say so."

REFRAIN

It's not easy to keep good news to yourself.

How to Answer Accusers

From the Songbook: Psalm 109:1–5, 26–31

They are my accusers, but I give myself to prayer. —Psalm 109:4

While I was a student at college, my roommate accused me of stealing $100 from him. He didn't confront me directly, but he spread his lie among his friends and reported it to the dean's office. The incident was thoroughly investigated, as it should have been.

It was the most helpless experience I have ever faced. All I could do was say, "I didn't do it." But those words seemed hollow against the accusation and rumor.

Inside *the* Song

In this psalm, David is facing deceitful and slanderous liars. His response? In the Hebrew the best translation is simply, "But I pray." Can we say that in similar circumstances?

I didn't know what to do. Part of me wanted to knock the truth out of my roommate. Another part wanted to contact all who heard about it and tell them I was innocent. Only later did my accuser admit that he had faked the theft to get money out of his parents for a stereo.

King David had a similar experience. Someone was making terrible accusations against him, undermining his position and causing him much grief (Psalm 109:2–4).

So what did David do? Did he use his authority to have his accuser killed? No, he prayed and asked the Lord to intercede, punish the slanderer, and make it right (vv. 4–29).

When someone spreads false rumors about us, we may want to retaliate. How much better it is to answer our accusers with the power of prayer!

—Dave Egner

REFRAIN

What matters more than what others say about us is what we say to God.

He Lights the Way

From the Songbook: Psalm 112

Unto the upright there arises light in the darkness; He is gracious, and full of compassion, and righteous. —PSALM 112:4

A missionary in Peru told of going one evening to visit a small group of believers. She knew that the house where they were meeting was located on a cliff and that climbing up the pathway would be treacherous. From her own house she took a taxi as far as it could go, and then she began the hazardous ascent to the house. The night was dark and the way was very difficult. As she rounded a bend, she suddenly came upon several believers carrying bright lanterns. They had come out to light the way. Her fears relieved, the missionary ascended the path easily and had a good meeting.

In a similar way, God lights our pathway. When we accepted Jesus as our personal Savior, He who is the Light of the world entered our lives and removed the darkness of our sin and despair. This light continues to comfort us through times of sorrow. In the midst of sadness, trouble, illness or disappointment, the Lord brightens the way and encourages His children by giving hope. This may come through a word of exhortation from a fellow believer. It may be the soothing illumination of His Word by the ministry of the Holy Spirit. It may be calm reassurance in response to heartfelt prayer. Or it may be the miraculous supply of a specific need. Whatever the case, God sends light when we are engulfed in darkness of the "valley of the shadow of death."

For the believer, there is always light in the darkest night!

—*Dave Egner*

Inside *the* Song

Many Christians in days past received hope from this line: "Unto the upright there arises light in the darkness."

♪ REFRAIN

When we need it most, the Light of the World shines into our lives.

I Love You, Daddy

From the Songbook: Psalm 116

I love the LORD, because He has heard my voice and my supplications.
—PSALM 116:1

Sincere and voluntary expressions of love make for close personal relationships. Nowhere is this more important than in our walk with God. It's one thing to go through the motions of obeying Him out of duty, but it's quite another to serve Him out of a genuine devotion and to tell Him often that we love Him.

The value of voicing our affection was emphasized to me by something my two-year-old daughter did. Although Katie had learned the mechanics of saying, "I love you" by mimicking Mom and Dad as we spoke to her, one evening her words took on special meaning. While we were playing together, she ran to me without prompting, put her little arms tightly around my neck and said, "I love you, Daddy!" That moment was so precious to me. Her words went straight to my heart because they were sincere, unrehearsed, and pure.

Reflecting on that incident, I'm reminded that the Lord desires the same kind of response from each of His spiritual children. As we contemplate what God does for us, we will begin to love and appreciate Him more and more. He gives us new life. He showers us with His favor. He disciplines us in love. He provides us with spiritual gifts to serve Him. And He's building an eternal home for us. When we realize that all these blessings are an expression of His love, we will be eager to show our own love for Him. Then we'll be ready to say, "Jesus, I love you!" Has He heard you tell Him that recently?

—*Kurt DeHaan*

Inside *the* Song

In verses 1–2, we get a great word picture. God leans over and puts His head near us so we can speak into His ear. What a warm picture of God's care for His child!

REFRAIN

Our prayer affords God another opportunity to shower His love on us.

In Brief

From the Songbook: Psalm 117

His merciful kindness is great toward us. —Psalm 117:2

I counted once and discovered that Abraham Lincoln's Gettysburg Address contains fewer than three hundred words. This means, among other things, that words don't have to be many to be memorable.

That's one reason I like Psalm 117. Brevity is its hallmark. The psalmist said all he had to say in thirty words (actually just seventeen words in the Hebrew text).

"Praise the LORD, all you Gentiles! Laud Him, all you peoples! For His merciful kindness [love] is great toward us, and the truth of the LORD [faithfulness] endures forever. Praise the LORD!"

Ah, that's the good news! Contained in this hallelujah psalm is a message to all nations of the world that God's "merciful kindness"—His covenant love—is "great toward us" (v. 2).

Think about what God's love means. God loved us before we were born; He will love us after we die. Not one thing can separate us from the love of God that is in Jesus our Lord (Romans 8:39). His heart is an inexhaustible and irrepressible fountain of love!

As I read this brief psalm of praise to God, I can think of no greater encouragement for our journey than its reminder of God's merciful kindness. Praise the Lord!

—*David Roper*

Inside *the* Song

Did you know that Paul quoted verse 1 in Romans 15:11? The psalmist, while writing to the Hebrew nation, was given a view of the faith that would include Gentiles as well, as Paul noted.

 REFRAIN

God's mercy extends to all who will accept His truth and His salvation.

A Bad Day?

From the Songbook: Psalm 118:15–24

This is the day the LORD has made; we will rejoice and be glad in it.
—PSALM 118:24

Dr. Cliff Arnall, a British psychologist, has developed a formula to determine the worst day of the year. One factor is the time elapsed since Christmas, when the holiday glow has given way to the reality of credit-card bills. Gloomy winter weather, short days, and the failure to keep New Year's resolutions are also a part of Dr. Arnall's calculations. One year, January 24 received the dubious distinction of being "the most depressing day of the year." It usually falls around that time.

Christians are not immune to the effects of weather and post-holiday letdown, but we do have a resource that can change our approach to any day. Psalm 118 recounts a list of difficulties including personal distress (v. 5), national insecurity (v. 10), and spiritual discipline (v. 18), yet it goes on to declare, "This is the day the LORD has made; we will rejoice and be glad in it" (v. 24).

The psalm is filled with a celebration of God's goodness and mercy in the midst of trouble and pain. Verse 14 comes as a shout of triumph: "The LORD is my strength and song, and He has become my salvation."

Even when circumstances hang a sign on our calendar saying "Bad Day!" the Creator enables us to thank Him for the gift of life and to receive each day with joy.

—*David McCasland*

Inside *the* Song

No wonder verse 24 is so encouraging. It is connected to verse 22, which looks ahead to our Savior's coming— "the chief cornerstone." The "day" in question was probably one of the Old Testament feast days.

 REFRAIN

When the Lord gave you this day, He expected you to do something great with it.

Follow the Signal

From the Songbook: Psalm 119:1–8

Oh, that my ways were directed to keep Your statutes! —Psalm 119:5

A driver who ignores traffic signals is "an accident looking for a place to happen." Anyone cheating on red or stopping absentmindedly on green is a danger to himself and to others. Although a series of red lights can be a pain when you're eager to get to your destination, an accident can bring even greater pain.

Several years ago I was happily surprised when a traffic signal was finally installed on a corner that had been especially frustrating to me. It turned a daily ordeal into an orderly and predictable way of getting onto a busy street. Waiting occasionally at a red light is now a pleasure—at least at that intersection of bad memories.

Inside *the* Song

Psalm 119 starts with obedience. We are to "walk in the law of the Lord" (v. 1), "keep His testimonies" (v. 2), and "do no iniquity" (v. 3). The goal? To keep God's "statutes."

The Scriptures too have some "red lights" that should control our lives as Christians. They are the prohibitions against envy, pride, hatred, irreverence, lust, and selfishness. When the Holy Spirit alerts us to their presence, we should immediately hit the brakes. Likewise, as we move into the heavy traffic of daily living, we must quickly respond by obeying the "green" signals of kindness, humility, love, worship, and purity.

God's stops and starts are designed to help us. We should be as fearful of ignoring a command of Scripture as we are of running a red light.

—*Mart DeHaan*

REFRAIN

Obedience leads to blessing; disobedience leads to danger, trouble, and regret.

From Heart to Heart

From the Songbook: Psalm 119:9–16

Your Word have I hidden in my heart, that I might not sin against You.
—Psalm 119:11

My childhood piano teacher was a stickler for memorization. Being able to play a piece without error was not enough. I had to play several pieces flawlessly by memory. Her reasoning was this: She didn't want her students to say, when asked to play, "I'm sorry, I don't have my music with me."

As a child, I also memorized Bible passages, including Psalm 119:11. Due to my limited understanding, I believed that simple memorization would keep me from sin. I worked hard at memorizing verses, and I even won a copy of *The Moody Bible Story Book* as an award.

Although memorizing the Bible is a good habit to develop, it's not the act of memorizing that keeps us from sin. As I learned soon after my winning efforts, having the words of Scripture in my head made little difference in my behavior. In fact, instead of victory over sin, knowledge alone generated feelings of guilt.

Eventually I realized that the Word of God had to spread through my whole being. I needed to internalize Scripture, to hide it "in my heart" the way a musician does a piece of music. I had to live the Bible as well as I could quote it. As God's Word spreads from our heads to our hearts, sin loses its power over us.

—*Julie Ackerman Link*

Inside *the* Song

Beginning in verse 9, young people are in focus. They are told to cleanse their ways through the Word. And in verse 11, a specific task is presented: memorizing Scripture. That too helps young people (and old) to avoid sin.

REFRAIN

The best place to keep your Bible is in your heart.

"I Dare You!"

From the Songbook: Psalm 119:41–48

And take not the word of truth utterly out of my mouth, for I have hoped in Your ordinances. So shall I keep Your law continually. —PSALM 119:43–44

I heard a story of a little church that was having a reunion. A former member who attended the celebration had worked hard and had become a millionaire. When he testified about how he had grown in the faith, he related an incident from his childhood.

He said that when he earned his first dollar as a boy, he decided to keep it for the rest of his life. But then a guest missionary preached about the urgent need on the mission fields. He struggled about giving his dollar. "However, the Lord won," the man said proudly, "and I put my treasured dollar in the offering basket. And I am convinced that the reason God has blessed me so much is that when I was a little boy I gave Him everything I possessed." The congregation was awestruck by the testimony—until a little old lady in front piped up, "I dare you to do it again!"

There's a vital truth behind that story. We must not let past attainments stop our spiritual growth. The psalmist said, "So shall I keep Your law continually." He knew he needed to keep his commitment fresh every day.

As Christians, we cannot rest on past attainments. We must give the Lord our full devotion now. Then no one will be able to say to us, "I dare you to do it again!"

—*Dave Egner*

Inside *the* Song

Living by the Book is an ongoing, everyday thing. To keep God's law continually allows us the special privilege, verse 45 says, of walking "at liberty," unencumbered by the problems that sin introduces into our lives.

🎵 REFRAIN

We can say that yesterday's spiritual victories were good, but today's challenge is to make sure we can say the same thing tomorrow.

The Forgotten Book

From the Songbook: Psalm 119:89–104

I will delight myself in Your statutes; I will not forget Your word. —Psalm 119:16

A young boy noticed a large black book all covered with dust lying on a high shelf. His curiosity was aroused, so he asked his mother about it. Embarrassed, she hastily explained, "That's a Bible. It's God's Book." The boy thought for a moment and then said, "Well, if that's God's Book, why don't we give it back to Him? Nobody around here uses it anyway."

In many homes, the Bible is hardly used or even thought about. The only time anyone picks it up to read it is when there's trouble, sickness, or a death in the family. And even then, the person may not know where to look for the help that's needed.

How long has it been since you've picked up your Bible and studied it for your own enjoyment, edification, and spiritual growth? Yes, it's God's Book—but He doesn't want it back. He wants you to keep it, to ponder it, to understand it, to believe it, and to obey its message.

That's the primary reason for the devotional guide *Our Daily Bread*, which has been produced since 1956. Each devotional article is intended to help you understand God's Word.

Did you read today's Scripture passage? If not, why not do so right now? Don't let the Bible become the forgotten Book in your home.

—*Richard DeHaan*

Inside *the* Song

How do we delight in statutes? Isn't that like getting excited about laws? It's a delight only if we find that living God's way of righteousness is better than living man's way of sin.

REFRAIN

Thinking of the joy provided by God's will and His standards helps us stay on the right side of lifestyle issues.

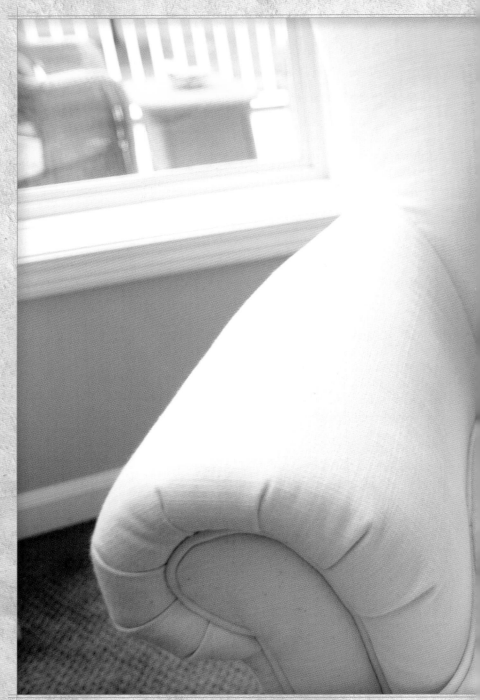

The Cheat Test

From the Songbook: Psalm 119:129–136

Direct my steps by Your word, and let no iniquity have dominion over me.
—PSALM 119:133

Dan Ariely, an economics professor at the Massachusetts Institute of Technology, conducted some tests on human behavior. In one experiment, the participants took an examination in which they would receive money for each correct answer. The participants didn't know, however, that Ariely was not testing their knowledge but whether they would cheat. He set up the test so that the groups thought it would be easy to get away with cheating.

Prior to taking the exam, one group was asked to write down as many of the Ten Commandments as they could remember. To Ariely's astonishment, none from this group cheated! But all the other groups did have those who cheated. Recalling a moral benchmark made the difference.

Centuries ago, the psalmist understood the need for a moral benchmark and asked for divine aid in following it. He prayed to the Lord, "Direct my steps by Your word, and let no iniquity have dominion over me. . . . Teach me Your statutes" (Psalm 119:133–135).

Ariely's "cheat test" experiment illustrates our need for moral guidance. The Lord has given us His Word as a lamp for our feet and a light for our path (v. 105) to direct us in our moral choices.

—*Dennis Fisher*

Inside *the* Song

Verse 134 tells us that letting "iniquity have dominion" over us leads to oppression. Choosing, instead, to get direction from God's Word leads to light (v. 130).

REFRAIN

Avoid moral decay; live God's way.

A Fair Trade

From the Songbook: Psalm 119:161–168

I rejoice at Your word as one who finds treasure. —Psalm 119:162

Scott and Mary Crickmore poured 15 years of their lives into helping to translate the New Testament in the Maasina dialect. It was for the Fulani tribe in the West African nation of Mali.

After the initial draft, Mary visited nearby villages and read it to people. She sat in huts with a group of men or women listening to them discuss what they understood. That helped her to make sure the words they were using in the translation were accurate and clear.

Some people would think that the Crickmores' sacrifice was too great—giving up their comfortable lifestyle, changing their diet to mush and rice, and living in less-than-ideal circumstances for those 15 years. But the Crickmores say it was "a fair trade," because now the Fulani people have the Word of God in a language they can read.

The psalmist delighted in God's Word. He stood in awe of it, rejoiced over it, loved it, and obeyed it (Psalm 119:161–168). He found great peace and hope in the Word.

The Fulani people are now able to discover the "great treasure" (v. 162) of God's Word. Would you agree with the Crickmores that any effort and sacrifice to get the Bible to others is "a fair trade"?

—Anne Cetas

Inside *the* Song

For a picture of the excitement of discovering God's Word, read 2 Kings 22:3–10. When the Book of the Law was discovered and read to the people, the kingdom of Judah was transformed.

REFRAIN

Is God's Word hidden in your house or in your heart?

Beyond the Shadows

From the Songbook: Psalm 121

I will lift up my eyes to the hills—from whence comes my help? —PSALM 121:1–2

I love the view of the Rockies from Denver. In the foreground are the foothills, and behind them are the high mountains. On a clear day, one can see Long's Peak, Mount Evans, and other peaks reaching altitudes of 14,000 feet, their tops covered with snow.

Early one morning, as I looked west to the mountains, I saw a sight that filled me with wonder. Because of a layer of low, gray clouds, the foothills lay in heavy shadows. Snow was probably falling. The foothills were dark and ominous, enough to discourage any potential traveler. But beyond them, the white, snow-capped peaks of the high mountains were glistening in the bright sunlight. They seemed to say, "Once you get through the shadows, you'll be all right."

As I looked at that sight, I thought how much it is like our spiritual journey. We are pilgrim followers of Christ. Ahead we may be able to see only the foothill shadows of hardship, illness, disappointment, and trouble. The way appears foreboding and difficult. But then we lift our eyes higher. There, gleaming afar in the sunlight, are the glorious mountain peaks of God's promises.

Where are you right now? In gloomy foothills, clouded in darkness? Don't despair. Keep moving upward. Sunlit mountain peaks lie just beyond.

—*Dave Egner*

> ## Inside *the* Song
>
> This is one of the songs of ascent—songs of pilgrims "going up" to Jerusalem to worship. They look up at the hills—hills that at times held pagan shrines ("high places" of the kingdom era)—and ask where their help originates. The answer in verse 2 is "from the LORD."

REFRAIN

The better our view of God, the brighter our future looks.

He Never Sleeps

From the Songbook: Psalm 121

He will not allow your foot to be moved; He who keeps you will not slumber.
—Psalm 121:3

Giraffes have the shortest sleep cycle of any mammal. They sleep only between 10 minutes and 2 hours in a 24-hour period and average just 1.9 hours of sleep per day. Seemingly always awake, the giraffe has nothing much in common with most humans in that regard. If we had so little sleep, it would probably mean we had some form of insomnia. But for giraffes, it's not a sleep disorder that keeps them awake. It's just the way God has made them.

If you think 1.9 hours a day is not much sleep, consider this fact about the Creator of our tall animal friends: Our heavenly Father never sleeps.

Describing God's continual concern for us, the psalmist declares, "He who keeps you will not slumber" (Psalm 121:3). In the context of this psalm, the writer makes it clear that God's sleepless vigilance is for our good. Verse 5 says, "The LORD is your keeper." God keeps us, protects us, and cares for us—with no need for refreshing. Our Protector is constantly seeking our good. As one song puts it: "He never sleeps, He never slumbers. He watches me both night and day."

Are you facing difficulties? Turn to the One who never sleeps. Each second of each day, let Him "preserve your going out and your coming in" (v. 8).

—*Bill Crowder*

Inside *the* Song

Throughout Israel's history, the people often worshiped pagan gods. These entities had human characteristics. For instance, they slept. It was important then for the people to be reminded that God will "neither slumber nor sleep" (121:4) as they traveled treacherous paths.

🎵 REFRAIN

A God who never sleeps should lead us to be followers who never fear.

Dying in the Service

From the Songbook: Psalm 122

I was glad when they said to me, "Let us go into the house of the LORD."
—PSALM 122:1

As a little boy was sitting in church, his eyes were attracted to a large flag bearing a number of gold stars. Turning to his father, he whispered, "Daddy, why does that flag have all those stars on it?" "To remind us of those who died in the service," was the reply. A puzzled look came over the boy's face. After thinking for a few moments about what his father said, he asked with childish innocence, "Daddy, did they die in the morning or evening service?"

We smile, yet the lad's misunderstanding suggests a sobering fact—many do "die in the service" every Sunday. I'm thinking about those who are turned off by the order of worship and find everything quite boring. They attend simply because it's the thing to do. As far as any spiritual benefit is concerned, they might just as well be dead.

The psalmist declared, "I was glad when they said unto me, 'Let us go into the house of the LORD.'" We know, of course, that when David referred to "the house of the LORD," he had Jerusalem in mind. Nevertheless, we should have the same attitude about going to church. When we enter our place of worship expecting a blessing, we'll receive one. You see, it's up to us. If we are faithful in attending a church where the Word of God is really believed and preached, if we go sincerely desiring the Lord's best, and if we have prayerfully prepared our own hearts, there will be no "dying in the service." Instead, the ministry of the Word, the singing of God's praise, and the fellowship of the Lord's people will bring spiritual health to our needy souls.

—*Richard DeHaan*

 REFRAIN

Seven days without church makes one weak.

Keep Laughing

From the Songbook: Psalm 126

Our mouth was filled with laughter, and our tongue with singing. —PSALM 126:2

A judge has ordered a German man to stop bursting into laughter in the woods. Joachim Bahrenfeld, an accountant, was taken to court by one of several joggers who say their runs have been disturbed by Bahrenfeld's deafening squeals of joy. He faces up to six months in jail if he is caught again. Bahrenfeld, 54, says he goes to the woods to laugh nearly every day to relieve stress. "It is part of living for me," he says, "like eating, drinking, and breathing." He feels that a cheerful heart, expressed through hearty laughter, is important to his health and survival.

A cheerful heart is vital in life. Proverbs 17:22 says, "A merry heart does good, like medicine." A happy heart affects our spirit and our physical health.

But there is a deeper, abiding joy for those who trust the Lord that is based on much more than frivolity and circumstances. It is a joy based on God's salvation. He has provided forgiveness of sin and a restored relationship with himself through His Son Jesus. That gives us a deep joy that circumstances cannot shake (Psalm 126:2–3; Habakkuk 3:17–18; Philippians 4:7).

May you experience the joy of knowing Jesus Christ today!

—*Marvin Williams*

Inside *the* Song

What was all the laughing about in verse 2? The people were beside themselves with joy because they had been released from captivity in Babylon and were allowed to return home. The Lord had indeed "done great things for them" (126:2).

♬ REFRAIN

There is no joy better than the joy of freedom—freedom from sin and eternal loss.

We All Need Mercy

From the Songbook: Psalm 130

With the LORD there is mercy, and with Him is abundant redemption.
—PSALM 130:7

I was reminded the other day that all of us need mercy. I read about a lady who stormed into a photography studio with a set of proofs and declared indignantly that they didn't do her justice. Looking her full in the face, the man behind the counter remarked wryly, "Lady, you don't need justice—you need mercy!" But don't we all? I remember many times in my own life when people acted graciously toward me. My parents, my teachers, my wife, my employers, and even the members of my former churches have often overlooked my failures. They've all treated me with loving kindness rather than harsh justice.

If we must have mercy from our fellowmen, how much more we need it from God! The words of Psalm 130:3 often come to my mind when I am alone in His presence: "If You, LORD, should mark iniquities, O Lord, who could stand?" How glad I am that He keeps on forgiving and forgiving.

As I write this devotional, I recall vividly the day I answered the telephone to hear a pastor friend on the other end of the line say, "My brother, do you know, 'it is because of the Lord's mercies that we are not consumed'?" Yes, I knew. I relied upon His grace when I received Christ, and His acceptance of me then was just the beginning of the goodness and favor He has been showering upon me ever since.

Have you acknowledged that you owe everything to God? Have you thanked Him for His kindly forbearance in forgiving you again, and again, and again? You should, because we all need mercy!

—*Herb Vander Lugt*

Inside *the* Song

Examine the beauty of this verse: "My soul waits for the Lord more than those who watch for the morning" (130:6). Indeed in God alone there is hope.

♪ REFRAIN

Without the soothing power of God's mercy, we would live in hopelessness.

Rained Out!

From the Songbook: Psalm 135:1–7

Praise the LORD! . . . He makes the lightning for the rain; He brings the wind out of His treasuries. —PSALM 135:1, 7

You have probably heard testimonies of how Christians prayed and the rain stopped just before an outdoor service began. Or perhaps it didn't start pouring until the final "Amen." Nowhere in the Bible, however, does God promise that He will always answer in such a dramatic way.

One autumn I was asked to speak at an outdoor evangelistic service at a county fair in Michigan. It was to begin at 2:30 p.m. The grandstands were full. A fine Christian high school choir was in place. We had prayed for the service, even as heavy, dark clouds were gathering. Then, just as the first hymn was announced, a violent storm swept through the fairgrounds. Swirling winds and driving rain lashed the grandstand. Lightning flashed and thunder roared. It wasn't long until we were forced to cancel the service. We were rained out!

Did this mean that God had lost control of His universe? Absolutely not! Were we out of His will for trying to hold an evangelistic service? No. It simply meant that at 2:30 that afternoon in Centreville, Michigan, God had different plans.

Whether God stops the rain or lets it pour, we can be sure that He is in control and He will do what is best. And we can praise the Lord for that.

—*Dave Egner*

Inside *the* Song

God's sovereignty, according to verse 7, extends even to the lightning, the rain, and the wind. The psalmist tells us that those things come from God's "treasuries," or storehouses.

REFRAIN

When circumstances seem to be spiraling out of control, remember God is still in control.

A Safe Pair of Hands

From the Songbook: Psalm 138

Your right hand will save me. —PSALM 138:7

Edwin van der Sar, goalkeeper for the Manchester United soccer team, had a "safe" pair of hands. He kept the ball from entering his team's goal for 1,302 minutes, a world record in one season! That means that for almost 15 games of 90 minutes each, no one was able to score even one goal against his team while he was guarding the goalposts. But one goal by an opposing team in March 2009 ended his record.

The psalmist David found comfort in the safest pair of hands— God's hands. He wrote of God's protection in Psalm 138, "You will stretch out Your hand . . . and Your right hand will save me" (v. 7). Like David, we can look to God's safe hands to keep us from spiritual danger and defeat.

Inside *the* Song

In Psalm 138, we hear the echo of Psalm 136:12. God did not want His people to forget that He had delivered them from captivity in Egypt.

Another assurance from God's Word for followers of Christ is Jude 1:24–25: "Now to Him who is able to keep you from stumbling, and to present you faultless before the presence of His glory with exceeding joy, to God our Savior, who alone is wise, be glory and majesty, dominion and power, both now and forever. Amen." That doesn't mean we'll never stumble. But it does mean we won't stumble so badly that God cannot pick us up.

God's safe pair of hands can never fail—ever!

—C. P. Hia

REFRAIN
You're always in good hands when you trust God.

Those Inner Flaws

From the Songbook: Psalm 138

The LORD will perfect that which concerns me. —PSALM 138:8

Most of us will admit that we have personality flaws and character weaknesses. We see undesirable tendencies in ourselves, such as selfishness, irritability, impatience, cruelty, vindictiveness, hotheadedness. They are with us because of our fallen sinful condition. Yet many Christians testify that their defects and weaknesses have become a blessing, causing them to rely more heavily on Jesus. By acknowledging their weakness, these believers have experienced God's grace and strength.

We can see this link between imperfection and improvement all around us in nature. Take, for instance, the formation of crystals, which make up our valuable minerals and precious stones. Scientists tell us that few things develop more orderly and predictably than crystals. Each kind of mineral and gem has its own special shape or appearance. In addition, every one of them is made up of a great number of atoms stacked in perfect alignment. Occasionally, though, one of these basic particles gets out of line. Surprisingly, these occurrences are essential steps in the development of crystals. They give them their most beautiful properties. Most gems owe their brilliant colors to these flaws.

Inside *the* Song

Notice David's reference to trouble in verse 7 and then the reminder of God's work in his life in verse 8. God accomplishes His work despite our humanity and failures.

Have you been worried about faults or shortcomings in your life? Don't let them get you down. Instead, admit their presence, commit them to the Lord in prayer, and trust Him to give you victory. The psalmist said, "The LORD will perfect that which concerns me."

—*Mart DeHaan*

 REFRAIN

God's power is greater than our failures; His plan, better than our missteps.

Communion on the Moon

From the Songbook: Psalm 139:1–12

If I ascend into heaven, You are there. —PSALM 139:8

Apollo 11 landed on the surface of the moon on Sunday, July 20, 1969. Most of us are familiar with Neil Armstrong's historic statement as he stepped onto the moon's surface: "That's one small step for a man; one giant leap for mankind." But few know about the first meal eaten there.

Buzz Aldrin had brought aboard the spacecraft a tiny communion kit provided by his church. Aldrin sent a radio broadcast to earth asking listeners to contemplate the events of that day and to give thanks.

Inside *the* Song

Ever try to hide from God? No matter where we go— even to the moon or to the remotest place on earth— God is there, desiring a personal relationship with us.

Then, in radio blackout for privacy, Aldrin poured wine into a silver chalice. He read, "I am the vine, you are the branches. He who abides in Me, and I in him, bears much fruit" (John 15:5). Silently, he gave thanks and partook of the bread and cup.

God is everywhere, and our worship should reflect this reality. In Psalm 139 we are told that wherever we go, God is intimately present with us. Buzz Aldrin celebrated that experience on the surface of the moon. Thousands of miles from earth, he took time to commune with the One who created, redeemed, and fellowshipped with him.

Are you far from home? Do you feel as if you're on a mountaintop or in a dark valley? No matter what your situation, God's fellowship is only a prayer away.

—*Dennis Fisher*

 REFRAIN

One of the best presents we could ever get is something that is always with us: God's omnipresence.

Wonderfully Made

From the Songbook: Psalm 139:13–18

Marvelous are Your works, and that my soul knows very well. —Psalm 139:14

While getting an eye exam recently, my doctor hauled out a piece of equipment that I hadn't seen before. I asked him what the device was, and he responded, "I'm using it to take a picture of the inside of the back of your eye."

I was impressed that someone had invented a camera that could do that. But I was even more impressed by what my doctor could learn from that picture. He said, "We can gather a lot of details about your current general health simply by looking at the back of your eye."

My doctor's comment amazed me. It is remarkable that a person's overall health can be measured by the health of the eye. What care the Lord has taken to place these details in the bodies He has created! It immediately brings to my mind the words of David, the psalmist, who reveled in God's creativity: "I will praise You, for I am fearfully and wonderfully made; marvelous are Your works, and that my soul knows very well" (Psalm 139:14).

The enormous complexities of our bodies reflect the genius and wisdom of our great Creator. The wonder of His design is more than breathtaking—it gives us countless reasons to worship Him!

—*Bill Crowder*

Inside *the* Song

Inside every soul are the truth of God's existence and the reality of His marvelous creation. Think for a moment about your body and the multitudes of ways God's creative power is seen in it.

REFRAIN

Our contemplation of the majesty and the glory of God's creation will take an eternity.

A Fresh Glimpse of Glory

From the Songbook: Psalm 145:1–13

I will meditate on the glorious splendor of Your majesty, and on Your wondrous works. —Psalm 145:5

Every summer, thousands of *Good Morning America* viewers cast their votes to select "The Most Beautiful Place in America." I was delighted when one year the winner was announced, and it was Sleeping Bear Dunes National Lakeshore in my home state of Michigan. Admittedly, I didn't expect the winning location to be in my own backyard. It reminded me of the time my wife, Martie, and I visited Niagara Falls. A man nearby watched our tourist behavior and quipped, "Ain't nothin' to it. I see it every day."

How easily we grow accustomed to our surroundings and dulled to things that are familiar—even places and experiences that once brought great delight. Although God's glory is clearly displayed all around us, sometimes the busyness of everyday life blocks our view. We take for granted His amazing work in our lives. We lose the wonder of the cross. We forget the privilege of being His child. We neglect the pleasure of His presence and miss the beauty of His creation.

I love the psalmist's declaration: "I will meditate on the glorious splendor of Your majesty, and on Your wondrous works" (Psalm 145:5). Let's take time today to meditate on God's "wondrous works" and get a fresh glimpse of His glory!

—*Joe Stowell*

Inside *the* Song

Literally, the phrase "glorious splendor" can be translated from the Hebrew to be "the glory of the splendor of the majesty." That's a great combination of descriptive words for us to meditate on!

REFRAIN

Contemplate the shining splendor of God's majestic creation.

Not Enough Stars

From the Songbook: Psalm 147

Sing to the LORD with thanksgiving. —Psalm 147:7

"I like to play with the stars," a little girl told her pastor one day when he came to visit her. She was bedridden due to a severe spinal deformity, and her bed was positioned so that she had a good view of the sky. She wanted it that way so she could see the stars at night. "You see, many nights I wake up and can't get back to sleep," she told the minister, "and it's then that I play with the stars."

Her pastor, curious about what she meant by that, asked, "How do you play with the stars?" The child answered, "I pick out one and say, 'That's Mommy.' I see another and say, 'That's Daddy.' And I just keep on naming the stars after people and things I'm thankful for—my brothers and sisters, my doctor, my friends, my dog." And on and on she went, until at last she exclaimed, "But there just aren't enough stars to go around!"

Do you ever feel that way when you think about the many blessings God has showered on you? Of course, you could never name all your material, physical, spiritual, temporal, and eternal blessings. But from time to time, it's good to remember with gratitude His many favors. As you do, like that little girl, you'll feel like exclaiming, "There just aren't enough stars to go around!"

—*Richard DeHaan*

Inside *the* Song

Psalm 146:2 seems to indicate that praising God is a lifetime proposition: "While I live I will praise the LORD." There's so much to praise, it would take that long to do it properly.

REFRAIN

No matter how long you sing God's glory, you will never run out of praises.

Hallelujah!

From the Songbook: Psalm 148

Let them praise the name of the LORD, for His name alone is exalted.
—PSALM 148:13

Recently I saw a television commercial that made it appear that fish and animals were singing "The Hallelujah Chorus." At first it seemed a bit absurd and even sacrilegious to see angelfish and brown bears mouthing the word *hallelujah*. But as I thought about it, a passage of Scripture came to mind.

Psalm 148 calls for everything in creation to praise the Lord.

Inside *the* Song

What does it take to give God adequate praise? Angels. Sun and moon. Stars. Heavens of heavens. Waters above the heavens. Sea creatures. Mountains. Kings and princes. Young men and maidens. The list goes on. That's what it takes.

Included in the invitation are "great sea creatures" (v. 7), "beasts and all cattle; creeping things and flying fowl" (v. 10). Not exactly the usual crowd in the choir loft or the congregation on Sunday morning!

As you read Psalm 148, count the number of different elements of God's creation that are invited to join in praising the Lord. Among them are angels, stars, sea creatures, mountains, trees, animals, kings and princes, men and women, young and old.

The psalmist cried out, "Let them praise the name of the LORD, for His name alone is exalted; His glory is above the earth and heaven" (v. 13). Is anyone or anything excluded from this invitation? It appears not.

On this day and throughout the year, may each of us answer this call to praise God in a joyful and lasting way. Let's join all creation in celebrating the greatness of our God!

—*David McCasland*

REFRAIN

It takes a universe to praise an almighty God.

A Lesson in Praise

From the Songbook: Psalm 148

Praise the LORD! —Psalm 150:1

Psalm 150 is not only a beautiful expression of praise, but it's also a lesson in praising the Lord. It tells us where to praise, why we're to praise, how we're to praise, and who should offer praise.

Where do we praise? In God's "sanctuary" and "mighty firmament" (v. 1). Wherever we are in the world is a proper place to praise the One who created all things.

Why do we praise? First, because of what God does. He performs "mighty acts." Second, because of who God is. The psalmist praised Him for "His excellent greatness" (v. 2). The all-powerful Creator is the Sustainer of the universe.

How should we praise? Loudly. Softly. Soothingly. Enthusiastically. Rhythmically. Boldly. Unexpectedly. Fearlessly. In other words, we can praise God in many ways and on many occasions (vv. 3–5).

Who should praise? "Everything that has breath" (v. 6). Young and old. Rich and poor. Weak and strong. Every living creature. God's will is for everyone to whom He gave the breath of life to use that breath to acknowledge His power and greatness.

Praise is our enthusiastic expression of gratitude to God for reigning in glory forever.

—*Julie Ackerman Link*

Inside *the* Song

Like a song that rises to a crescendo, Psalm 150 ends the Psalms with a glorious musical climax as the instruments strain to glorify God.

REFRAIN

Let everything that has breath praise the Lord. Praise the Lord!

OUR DAILY BREAD WRITERS

Henry Bosch
The first editor of *Our Daily Bread*, Henry loved to sing—and actually did some recording for Radio Bible Class in its early years.

Dave Branon
An editor with Discovery House Publishers, Dave has been involved with *Our Daily Bread* since the 1980s. He has written several books, including *Beyond the Valley* and *Stand Firm*, both Discovery House publications.

Anne Cetas
After becoming a Christian in her late teens, Anne was introduced to *Our Daily Bread* and began reading it right away. Now she reads it for a living as the managing editor of *Our Daily Bread*.

Bill Crowder
A former pastor who is now an associate teacher for RBC Ministries, Bill travels extensively as a Bible conference teacher, sharing God's truths with believers in Malaysia and Singapore and other places where RBC has international offices.

Dennis DeHaan
When Henry Bosch retired, Dennis became the second managing editor of *Our Daily Bread*. A former pastor, he loved preaching and teaching the Word of God.

Kurt DeHaan
A grandson of Dr. M. R. DeHaan, Kurt was the managing editor of *Our Daily Bread* for several years. He held that position in the late summer of 2003 when he died of a heart attack at age fifty while enjoying his customary lunchtime jog.

Mart DeHaan
The former president of RBC Ministries, Mart followed in the footsteps of his grandfather M. R. and his dad, Richard, in that capacity. Mart, who has long been associated with *Day of Discovery* as host of the program from Israel, is now senior content advisor for RBC.

Richard DeHaan

Son of the founder of RBC Ministries, Dr. M. R. DeHaan, Richard was responsible for the ministry's entrance into television. Under his leadership, *Day of Discovery*, the ministry's long-running TV program, made its debut in 1968.

Dave Egner

A retired RBC editor and longtime *Our Daily Bread* writer, Dave was also a college professor during his working career. In fact, he was a writing instructor for both Anne Cetas and Julie Ackerman Link at Cornerstone University.

Dennis Fisher

As a research editor at RBC Ministries, Dennis uses his theological training to guarantee biblical accuracy. He is also an expert in C. S. Lewis studies.

Vernon Grounds

A longtime college president (Denver Seminary) and board member for RBC Ministries, Vernon's life story was told in the Discovery House book *Transformed by Love*.

C. P. Hia

A resident of Singapore, C. P. has been a men's Bible study leader for the past twenty years, and he also volunteers his services in the RBC Ministries office in his homeland—the only island city-state in the world. He has written for *Our Daily Bread* since 2008.

Cindy Hess Kasper

An editor for the RBC publication *Our Daily Journey*, Cindy began writing for *Our Daily Bread* in 2006.

Julie Ackerman Link

A book editor by profession, Julie has written for *Our Daily Bread* since 2000. Her book *Above All, Love* was published in 2008 by Discovery House.

David McCasland

A resident of Colorado, David enjoys the beauty of God's grandeur as displayed in the Rocky Mountains. An accomplished biographer, David has written several books, including *Oswald Chambers: Abandoned to God* and *Eric Liddell: Pure Gold*.

Our Daily Bread Writers

Haddon Robinson

Haddon has taught hundreds of young pastors the art of preaching. He is former president of Denver Seminary and served for many years as a professor at Gordon-Conwell Theological Seminary.

David Roper

David lives in Idaho, where he takes advantage of the natural beauty of his state. He has been writing for *Our Daily Bread* since 2000, and he has published several successful books with Discovery House Publishers.

Jennifer Benson Schuldt

Chicagoan Jennifer Schuldt writes from the perspective of a mom of a growing family. She has written for *Our Daily Bread* since 2010, and she also pens articles for another RBC publication, *Our Daily Journey*.

Joe Stowell

As president of Cornerstone University, Joe stays connected to today's young adults in a leadership role. A popular speaker and a former pastor, Joe has written a number of books over the years, including *Strength for the Journey* and *Jesus Nation*.

Herb Vander Lugt

For many years, Herb was the research editor at RBC Ministries, responsible for checking the biblical accuracy of the booklets published by RBC. A World War II veteran, Herb spent several years as a pastor before his RBC tenure began.

Paul Van Gorder

A writer for *Our Daily Bread* in the 1980s and 1990s, Paul was a noted pastor and Bible teacher—both in the Atlanta area where he lived and through the *Day of Discovery* TV program.

Marvin Williams

Marvin's first foray into RBC Ministries came as a writer for *Our Daily Journey*. In 2007, he penned his first *Our Daily Bread* article. Marvin is pastor of a church in Lansing, Michigan.

NOTES

Note to the Reader

The publisher invites you to share your response to the message of this book by writing Discovery House Publishers, P.O. Box 3566, Grand Rapids, MI 49501, U.S.A. For information about other Discovery House books, music, videos, or DVDs, contact us at the same address or call 1-800-653-8333. Find us on the internet at dhp.org or send an e-mail to books@dhp.org.